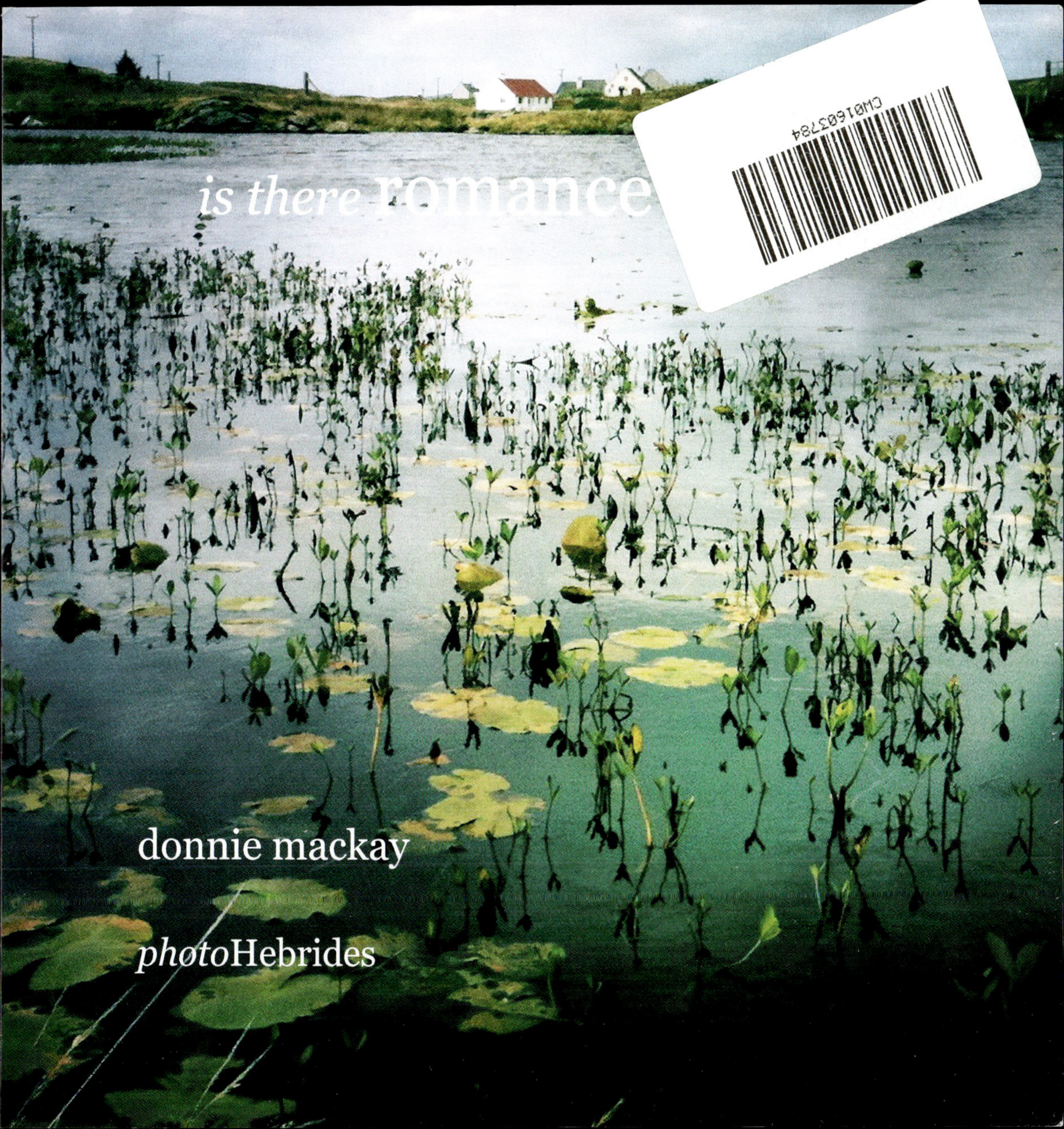

is there romance

donnie mackay

*photo*Hebrides

Published by *photo*Hebrides 2013

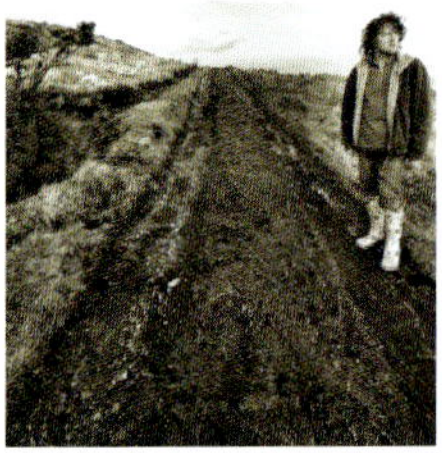

ISBN 978-0-9562184-3-8

Donnie Mackay is an archaeologist and photographer from the Isle of Skye in Scotland.

The book has been designed by the author using Blurb's BookSmart software and it was printed in The Netherlands. It is published by *photo*Hebrides - a small publisher based in Elgol, Isle of Skye, Scotland..

Donnie Mackay's other works include:

The Hebrides: A Geography of Time 2009
On a Grey Day: Photographs of the Hebrides 2011
The Road to Elgol 2011

(photohebrides@btinternet.com)

in that indefinite, delicately hesitant moment
between architecture and archaeology
time allows the shifting shadows to dance
a final chance
that fading walls might recuperate, revive and bloom
and sing to a new tune
a cheerful song
of romance in ruin

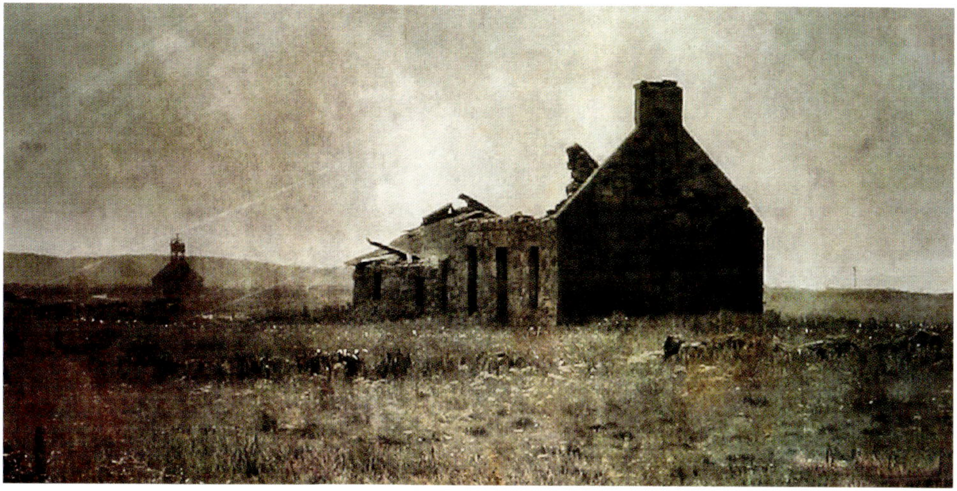

blog: www.photohebrides.org.uk

print sales: www.photohebrides.co.uk

54 of 200

there is no romance in ruin
no antiseptic
no silent staring, no sweet domestic
no giggling moment
no hand-holding torment
no sense of timeless joy
no love-crazed girl, no love-starved boy?

no?
no wild sense of love ... just loss
a loss of life
a loss of soul
a loss of memory
just heartache, absence, cold
no memories of that final dance
no last chance
no going back
no romance?

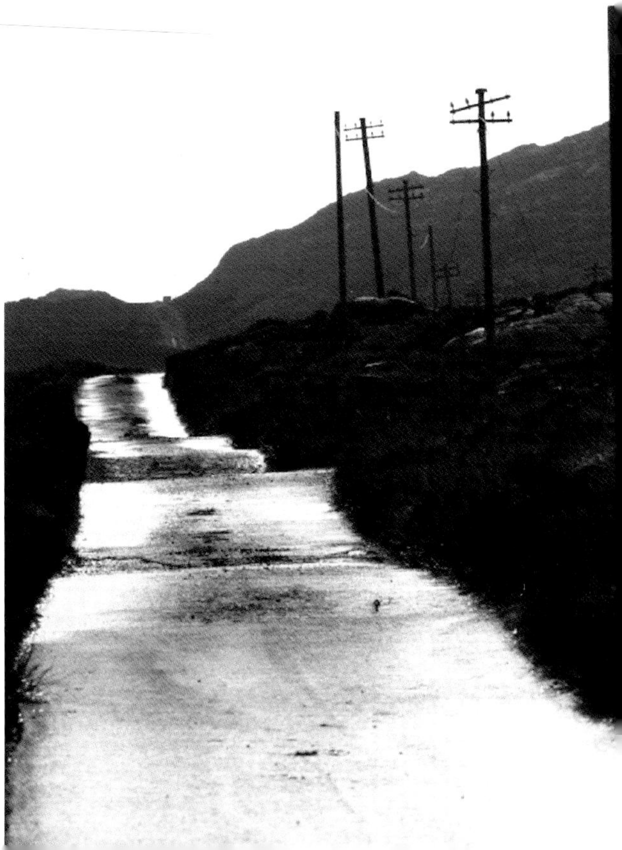

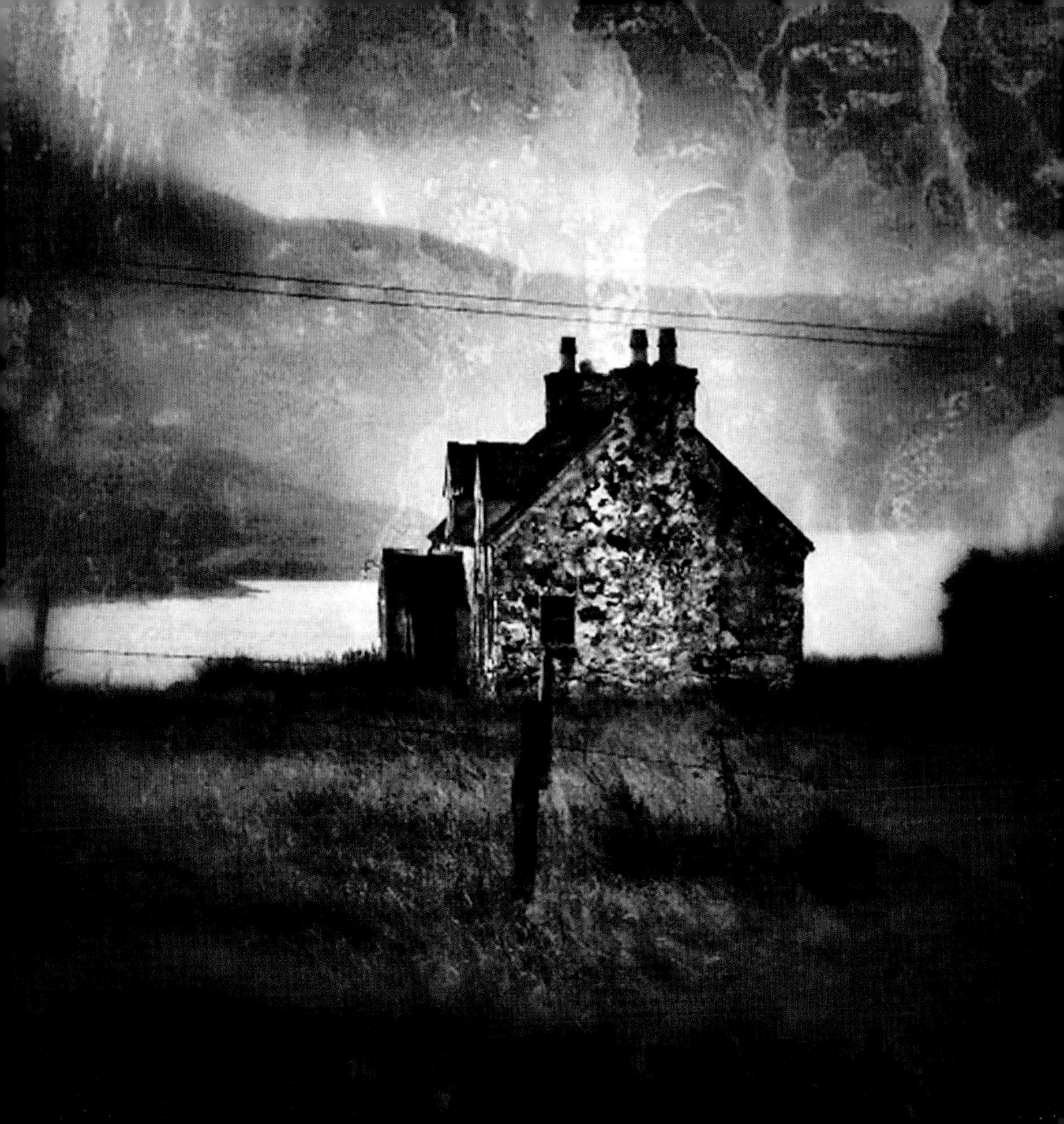

it was hot, unusually so
and when i sat on the flat welcoming rock
at the south side of the unassuming, bashful iron age hut
i had no thought that i might sit on an adder

to be precise
i did not think of an adder at all
until i sat down
beside one

at this reunion
this collision of senses and geology
this unification and juxtaposition of sentiment and time
i recalled the grass snake
at Invergarry
i was five years old
by coincidence that too was a snake, that i did not sit on

i remained, sitting, beside my second "adder"
with poorly disguised unease
the snake itself was idle in its disconcerting eloquence,
refined and mischievously calm

sunbathing
with total disregard for the great antiquity of its temporary bed
and further disregard
for its temporary disheveled acquaintance

i knew i should just return to my survey
but sunbathing snakes have power beyond their menacing dreams
power to distract those who dare to measure
who dare to interpret
and tell stories,
of passing places in time

i quickly finished my drawing of the increasingly forlorn, dissatisfied and disappointingly unstratified,
house

i realised then that there was romance and mystery, darkness and a charming malevolence of disputed
communication, in and around ruin

i finished quickly, and whispered an unconvincingly jaunty goodbye to my aloof friend
and struggled onwards in the early April sun

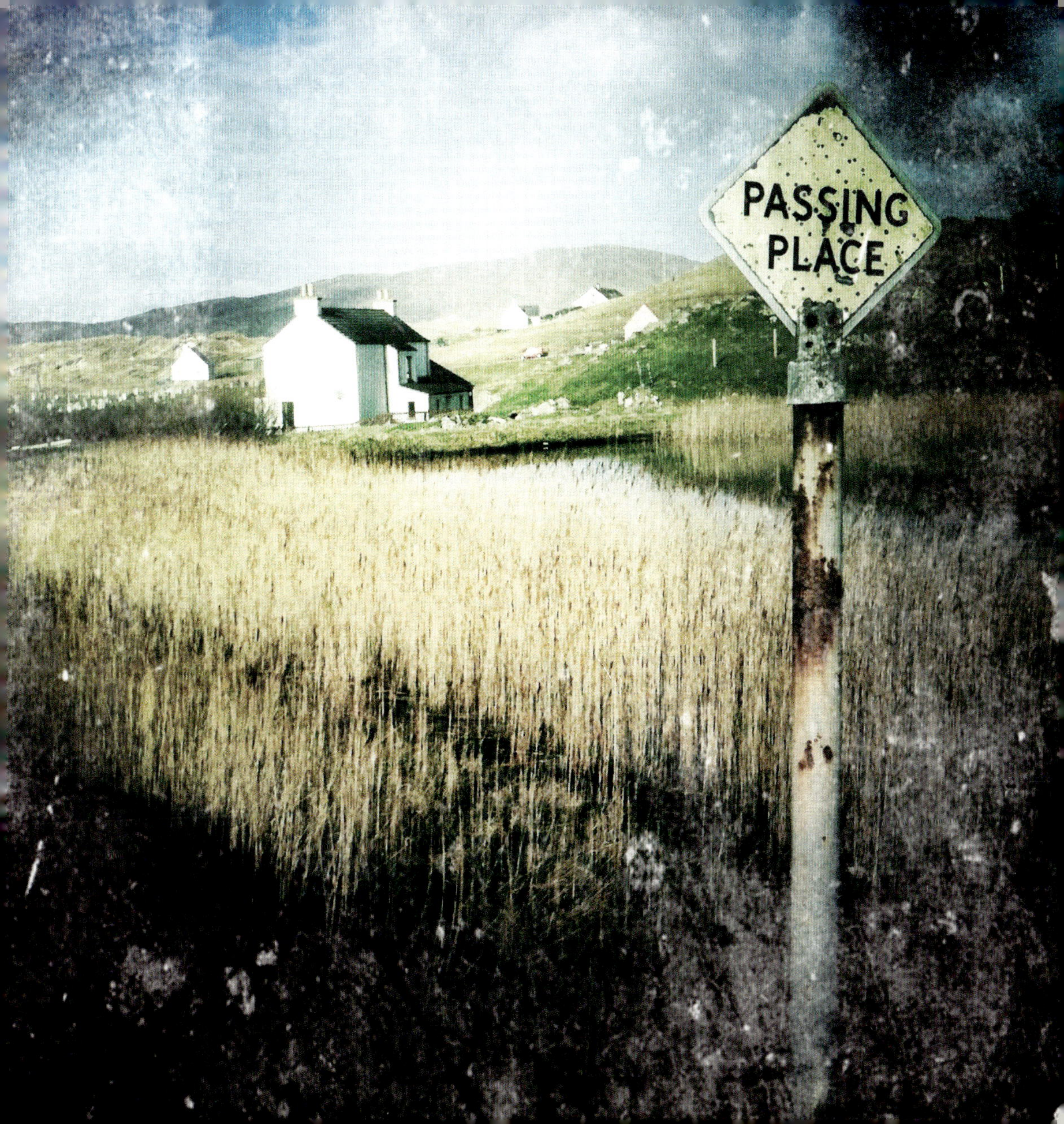
PASSING
PLACE

is there romance in ruin?

i stood at the gate and listened

the robin turned his head
curiosity defeating concern
and he too,
listened

we heard footsteps
faint and fading

delicate paths
across the floorboards
of a forgiving mind

behind the hidden outhouse door
giggling whispers and the echoes of slippered childhood feet
played hide and seek with emotion
kindling devotion to memories, scraped and rescued from a compacted, resilient floor

and, forever by my side
a small heart
determinedly beating
echoing irrepressibly
in the cold wind

a lingering repetitive movement
a delicate soul
tapping its memories
with a morse code of authority

an insistence on resistance
an unforgettable alarm
resonating its message

of good
of charm
of hope
not harm

we stood at the gate and listened

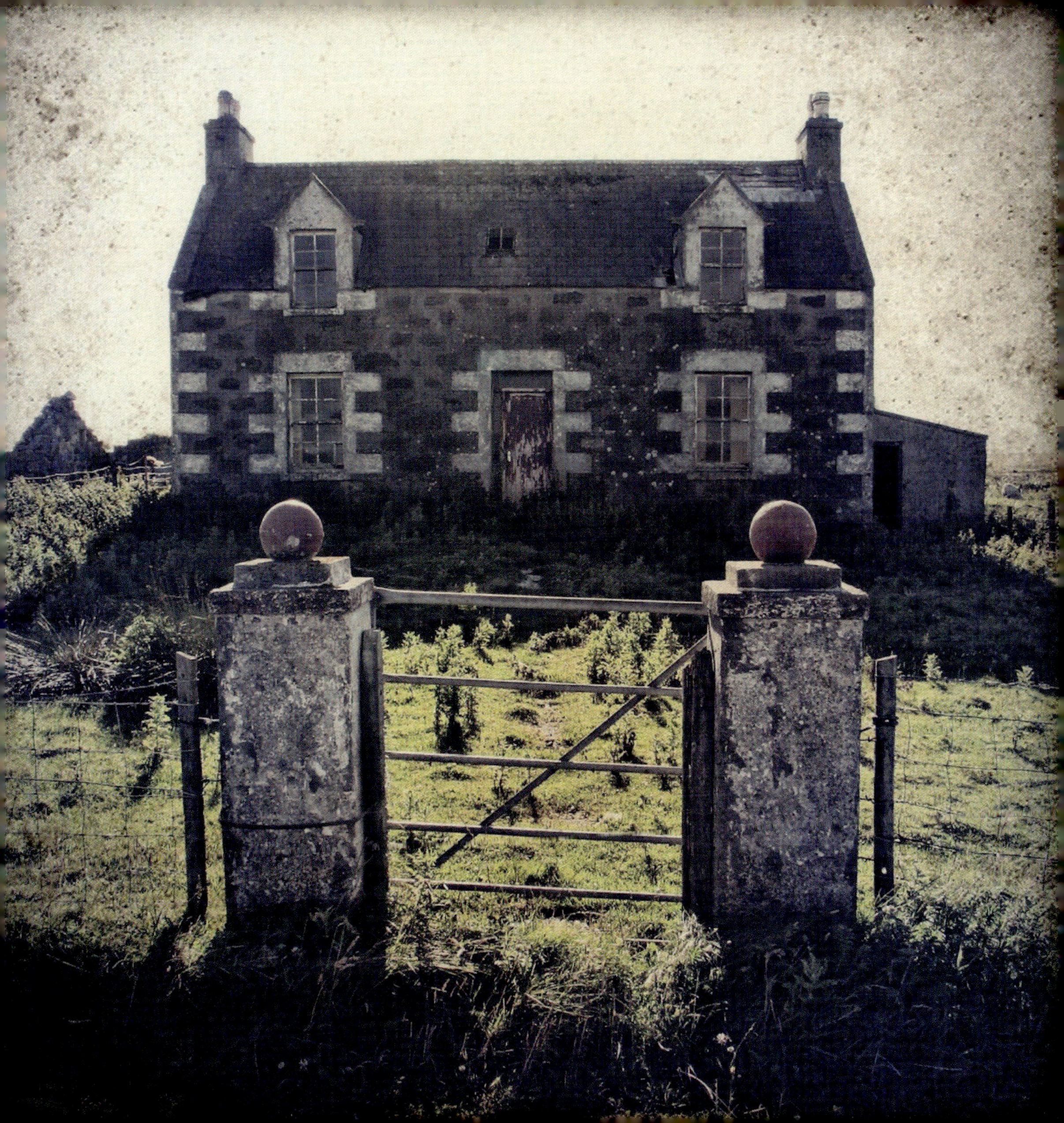

is there romance in ruin?

they were ornamental
primary
geometrically fundamental
unrealistically false coloured sentimental
the stars
and the moon
and the maddening orbs of
an estranged daylight
bludgeoning charismatic shadows without fright
yet challengingly captivating
stealthily unveiling the cloak
and the hidden dagger
of the northern night

was it ever a good intention?
to suggest that
to dream of
orchestral intervention

to imagine an art deco flurry
devoid of architecturally aesthetic worry

was an appropriate response to the questions of
how and when
who and why?

can we endorse emotion delivered from a contemplative lunar sky
painted energetically on the fabric of the mind
and written in the annals with a knowing
unregulated and unrepentant sigh?

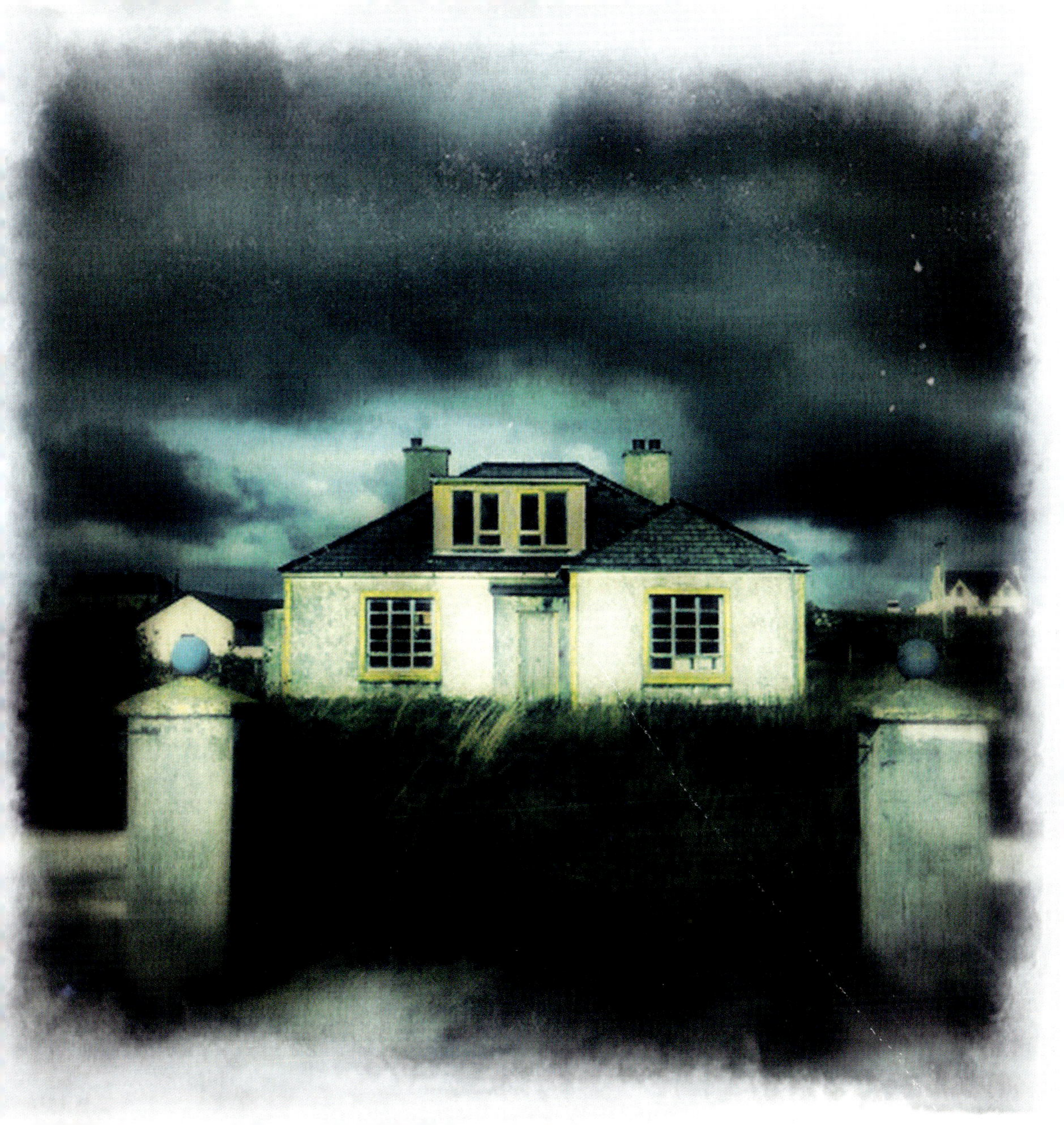

our old grey horse
dragged
the coarse beach sand and time-rounded pebbles
from the shore

we orchestrated the salty mix
under the light of a hot spring
misted with whisky

we shuttered the shore born mixture
with water and cement
and built our new bunker
our homely post-war walls

timbers patterned by the salty mix
still tell beach stories in the tileless loft

the home is now empty of people
but it is truly a solid box of dreams
and the creation mist is
trapped, stratified
in empty bottles under the floorboards
with the horseshoes
and the memories

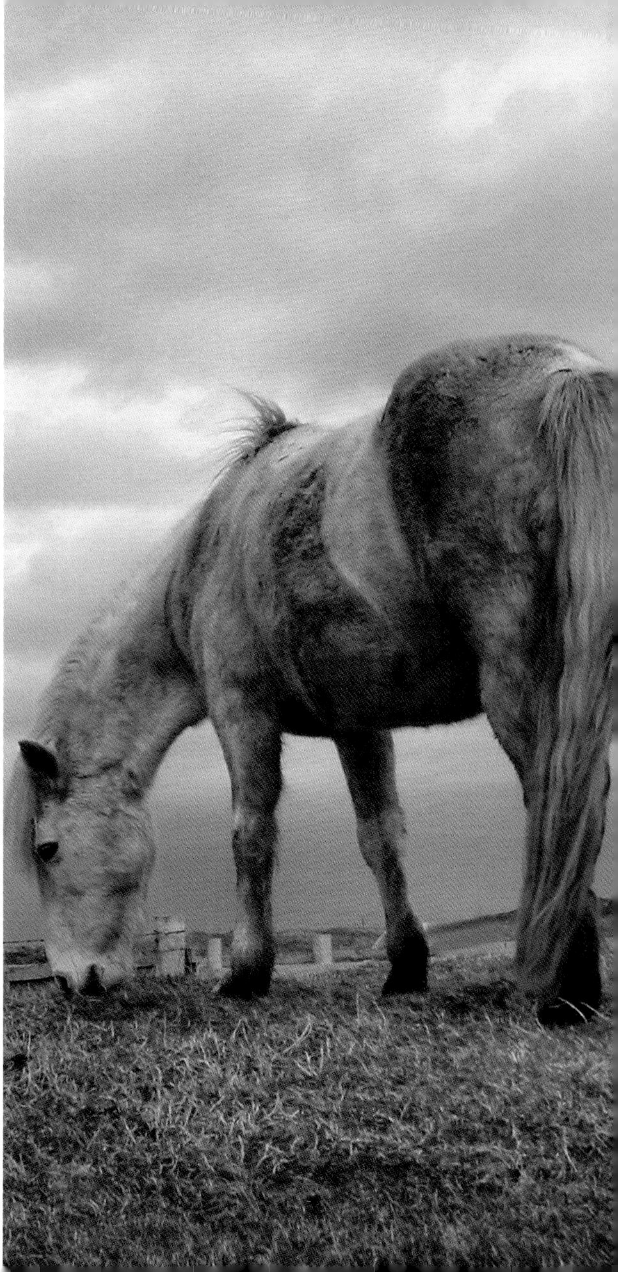

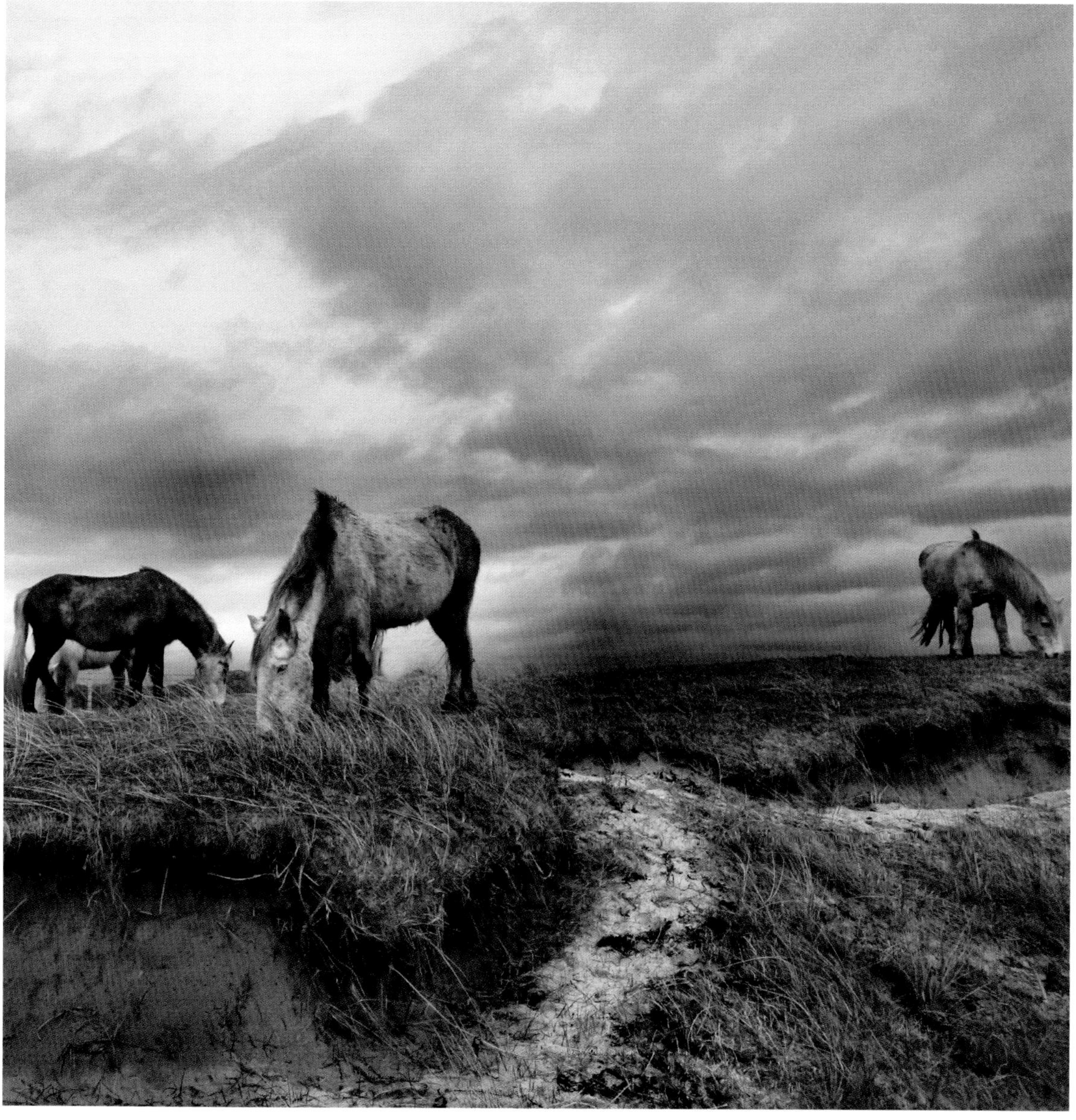

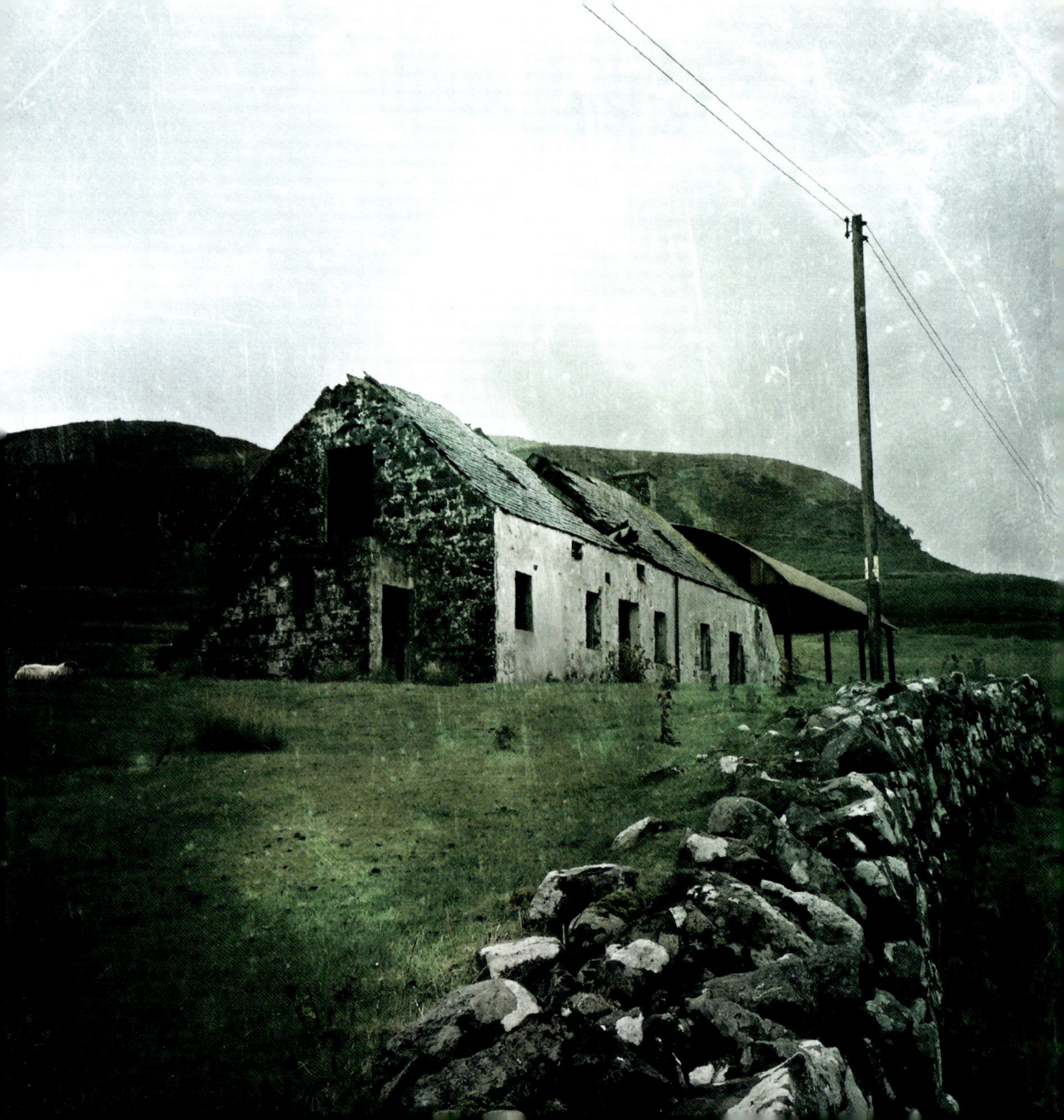

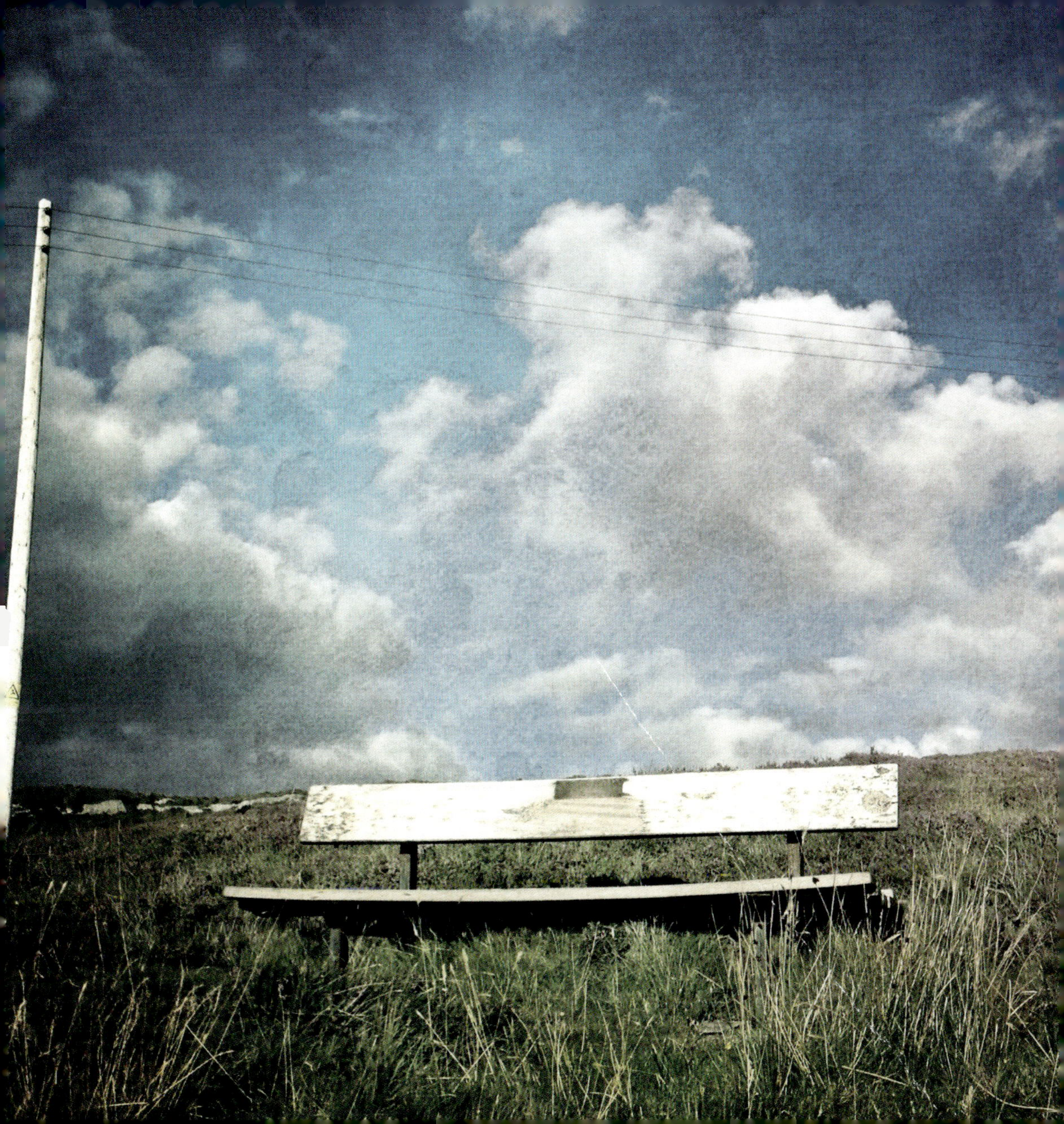

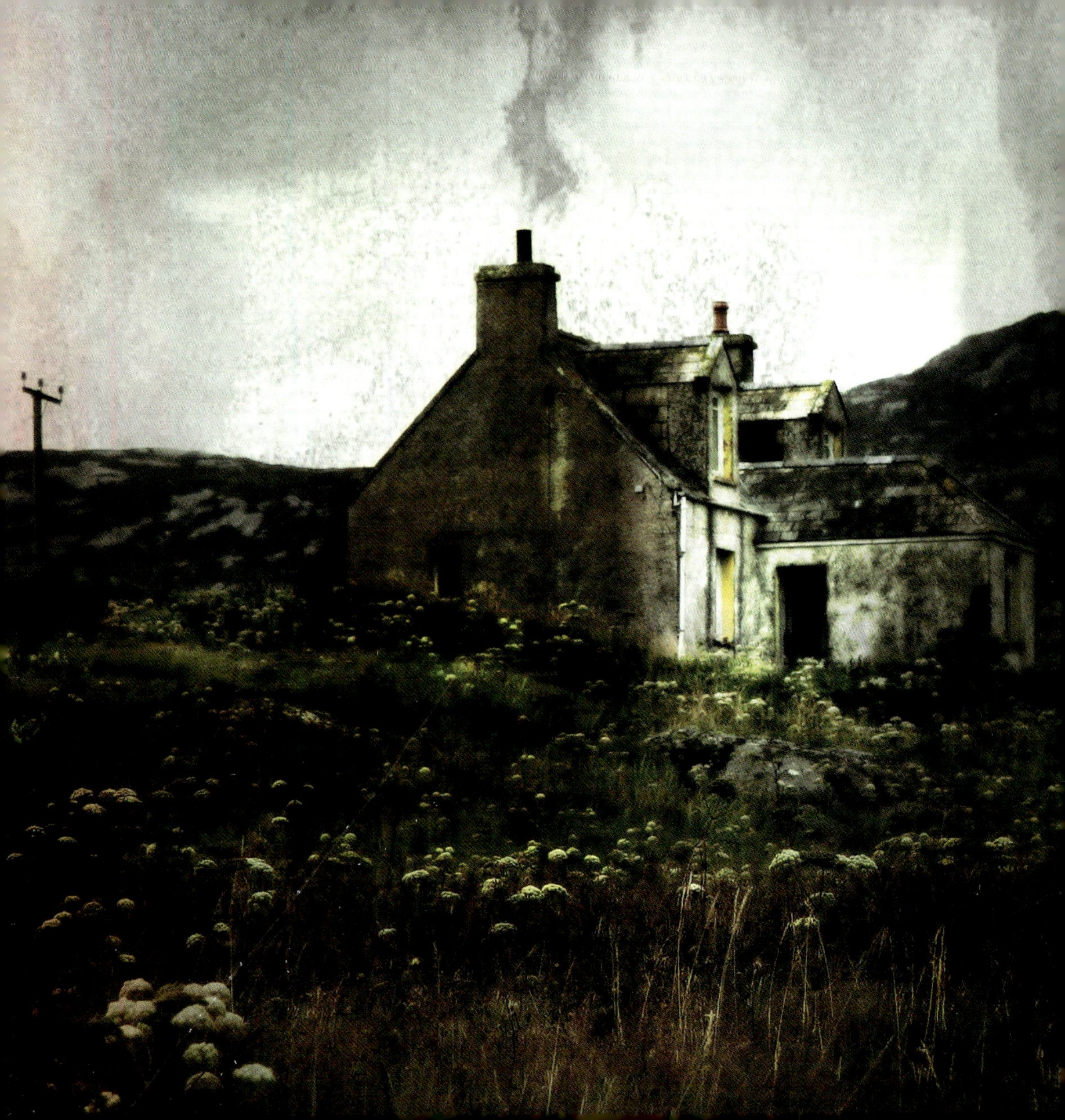

it was many years after
that the sun made its return
dancing keenly
through a little window in the western wall

a friendly enchanting curiosity
began the conversation

rays of optimism
sparkled and kindly teased
in the gentle invigorating glow
translating
pulsating
navigating
the language gap

light from this new dawn
deconstructed the staid secretly serendipitous
demeanor
of the stony face

and the masks and hesitations of time
were unveiled and uncovered
the anguish of the windswept years
evaporated

the revival had begun
the window onto a new world
was open
the ghosts
the opportunities
the ambassadors of different times
and different spaces
met, smiled and joined hands
at the passing place
of time

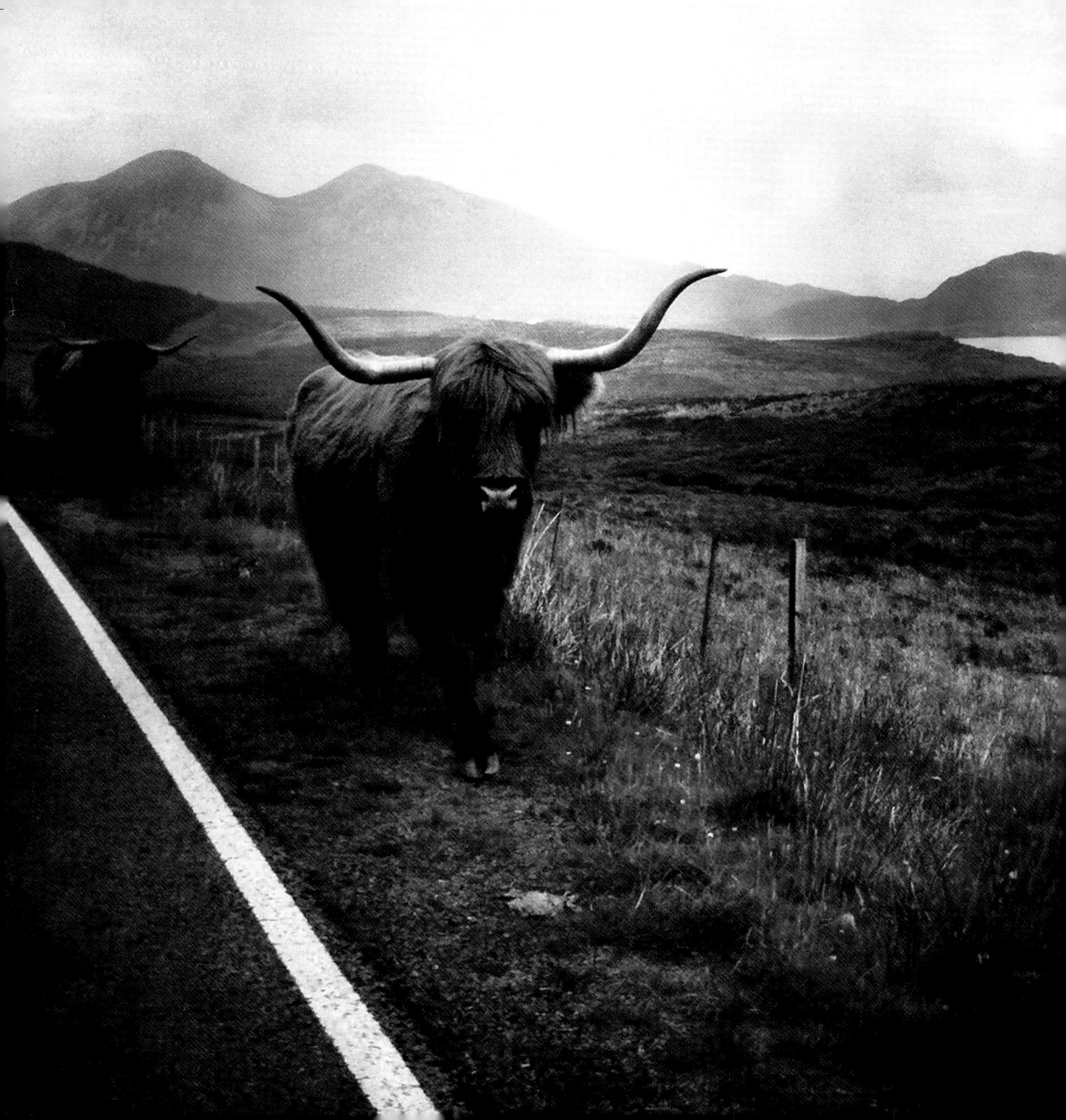

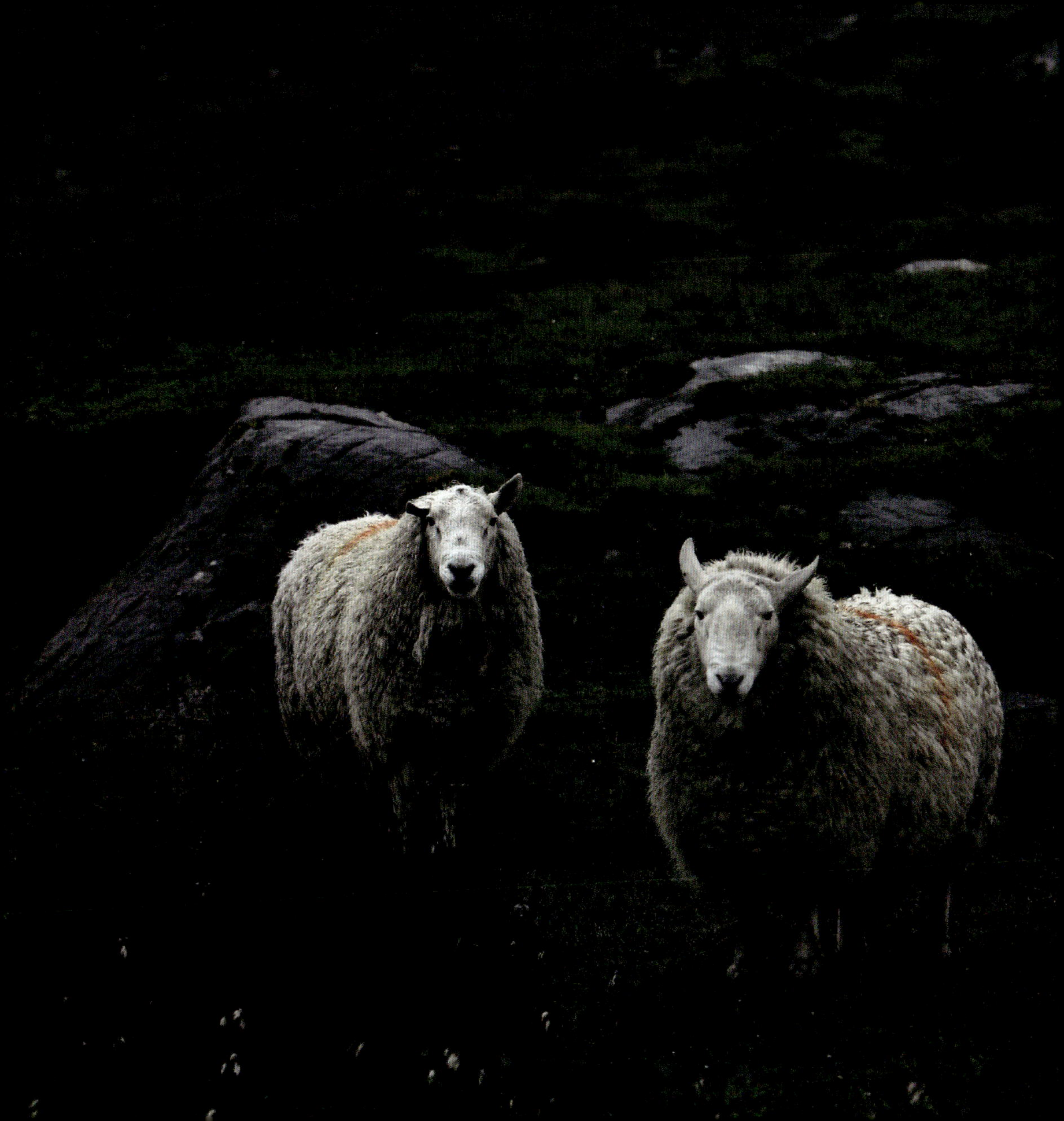

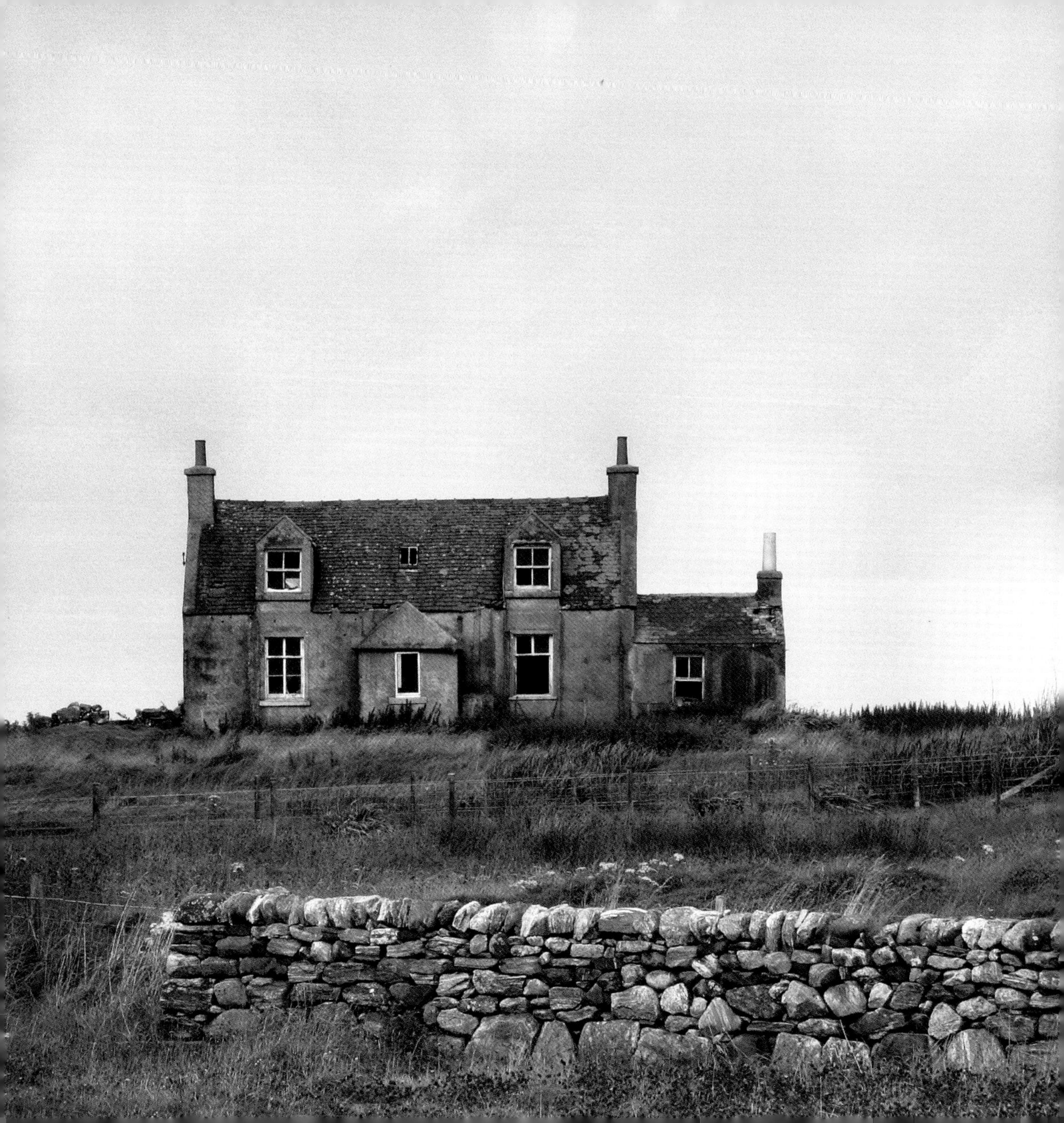

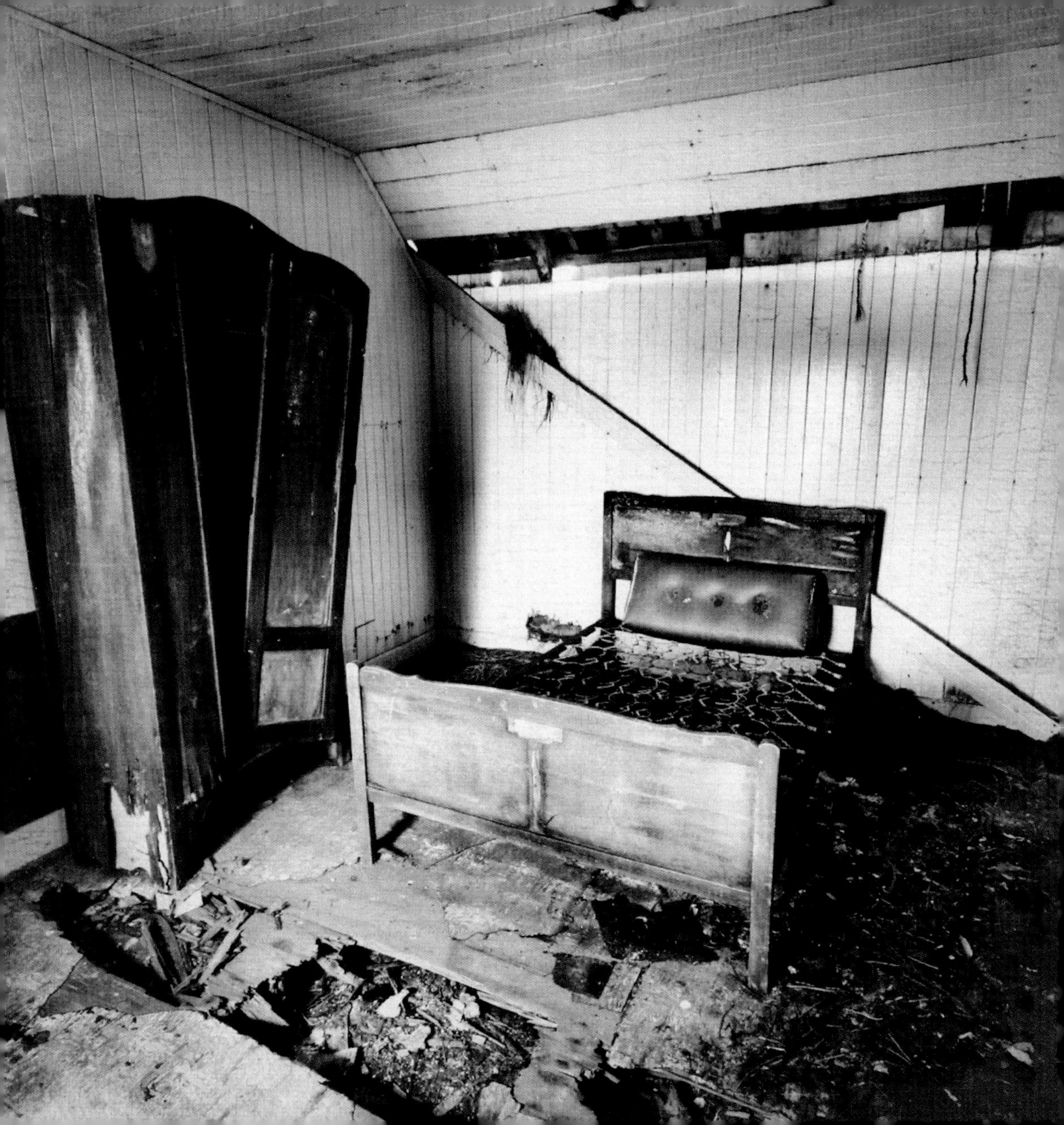

is there romance in ruin?

in November the blacksmith left the village
his fire reddened coals
stamped
and scattered in the trampled earth
of my sister's mind
smeared on the rooftop of her despair
a final belligerent flourish
of red

in the corner of the room
she hid
from the gossip
unkind
maligned

she prayed
and her heart
bled

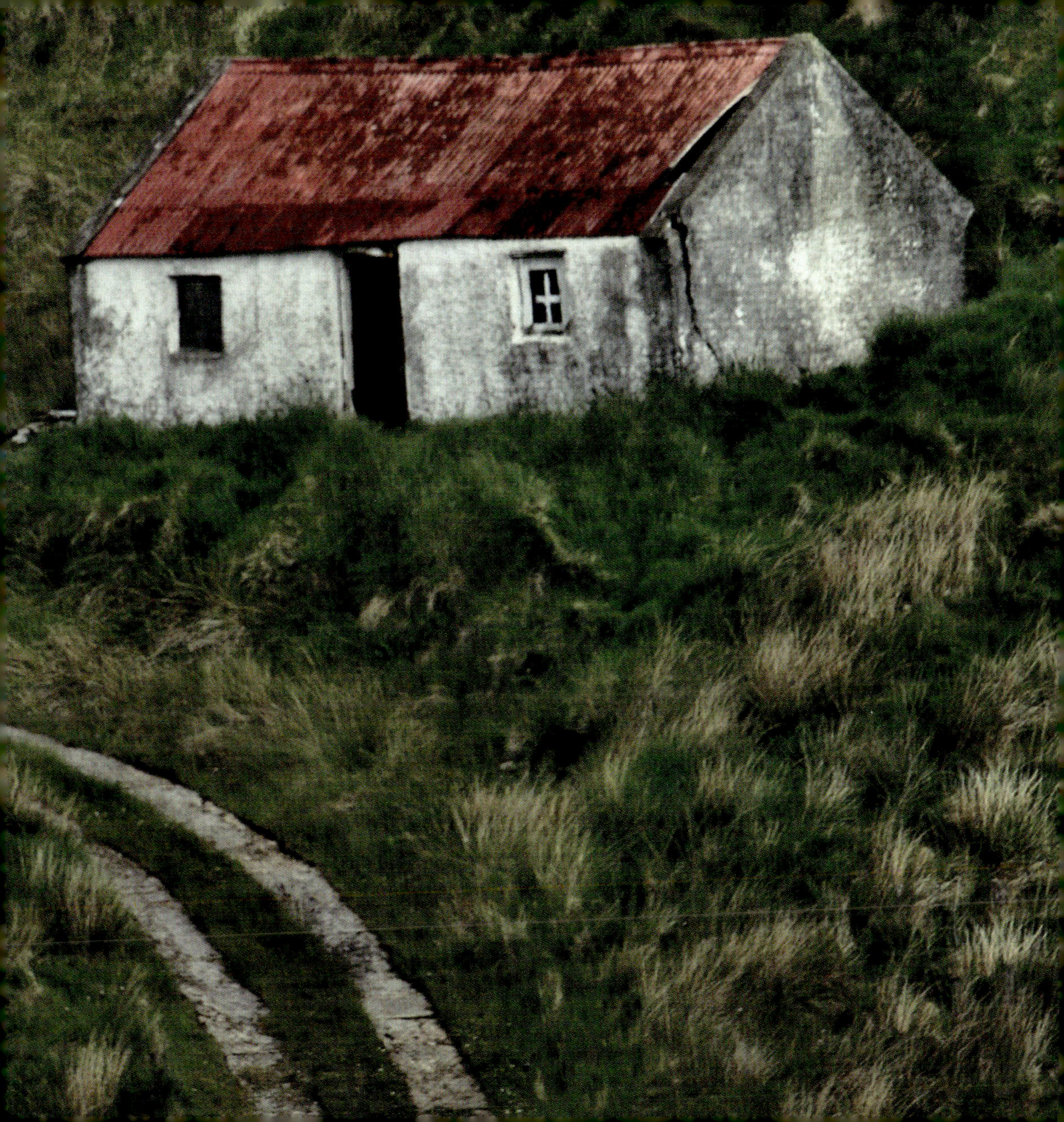

is there romance in ruin?

the slates whistled
their resistance loosened
resolve, fading and failed
losing a final grip on reality
with a precocious
tempestuously talented tap dance
across the roof
sailing into the chorus of the bellicose orchestral wind
with a final bombastic tone
of defiance
an exuberant mime
shouting
nine nine nine
measuring mood
and madness
momentum
and time

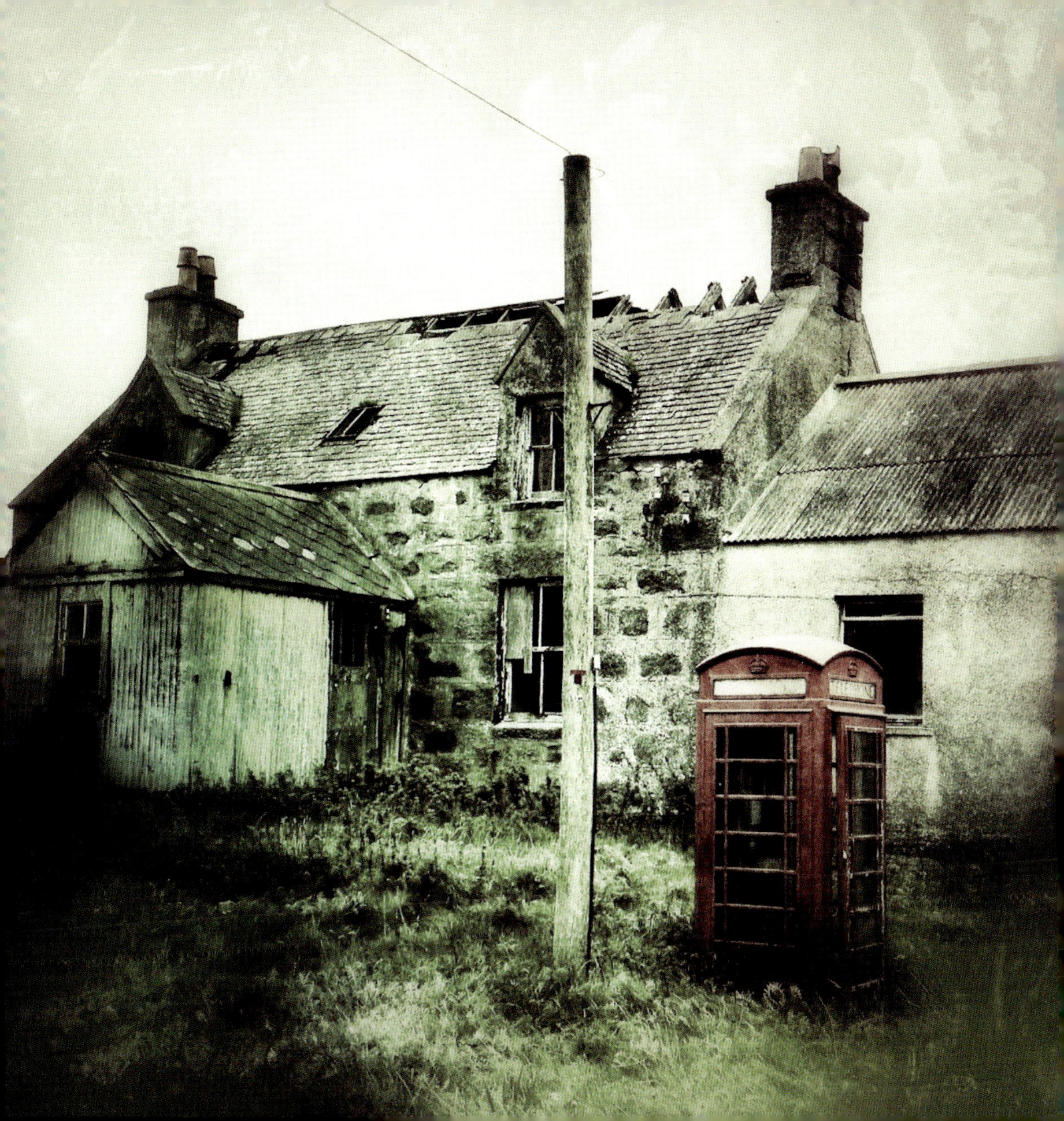

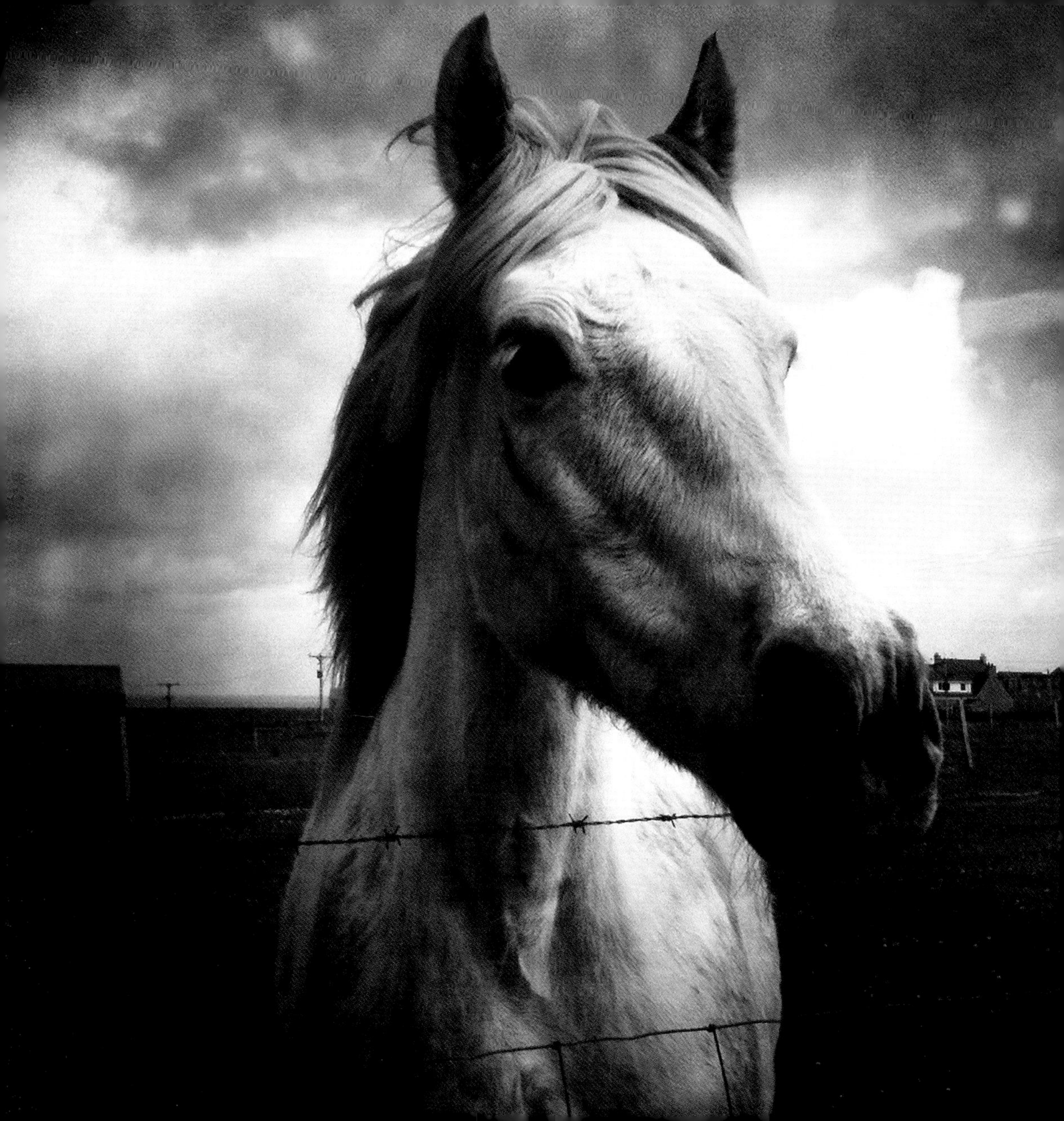

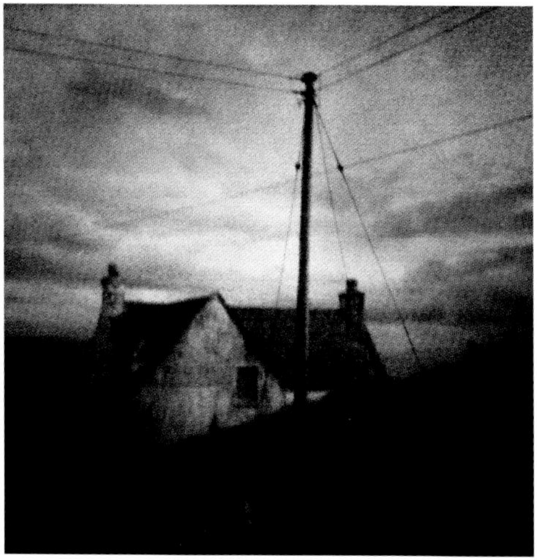

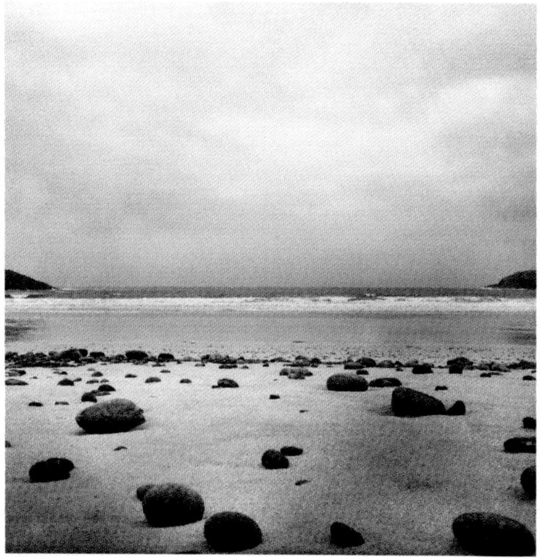

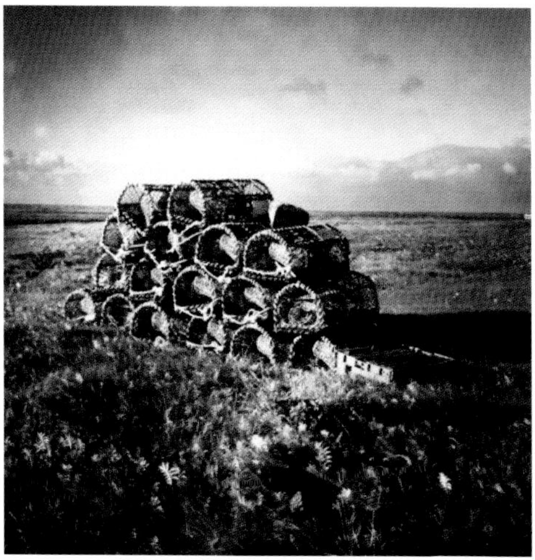

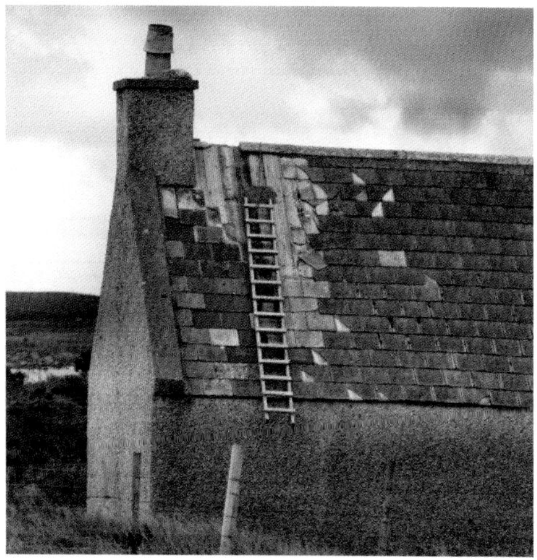

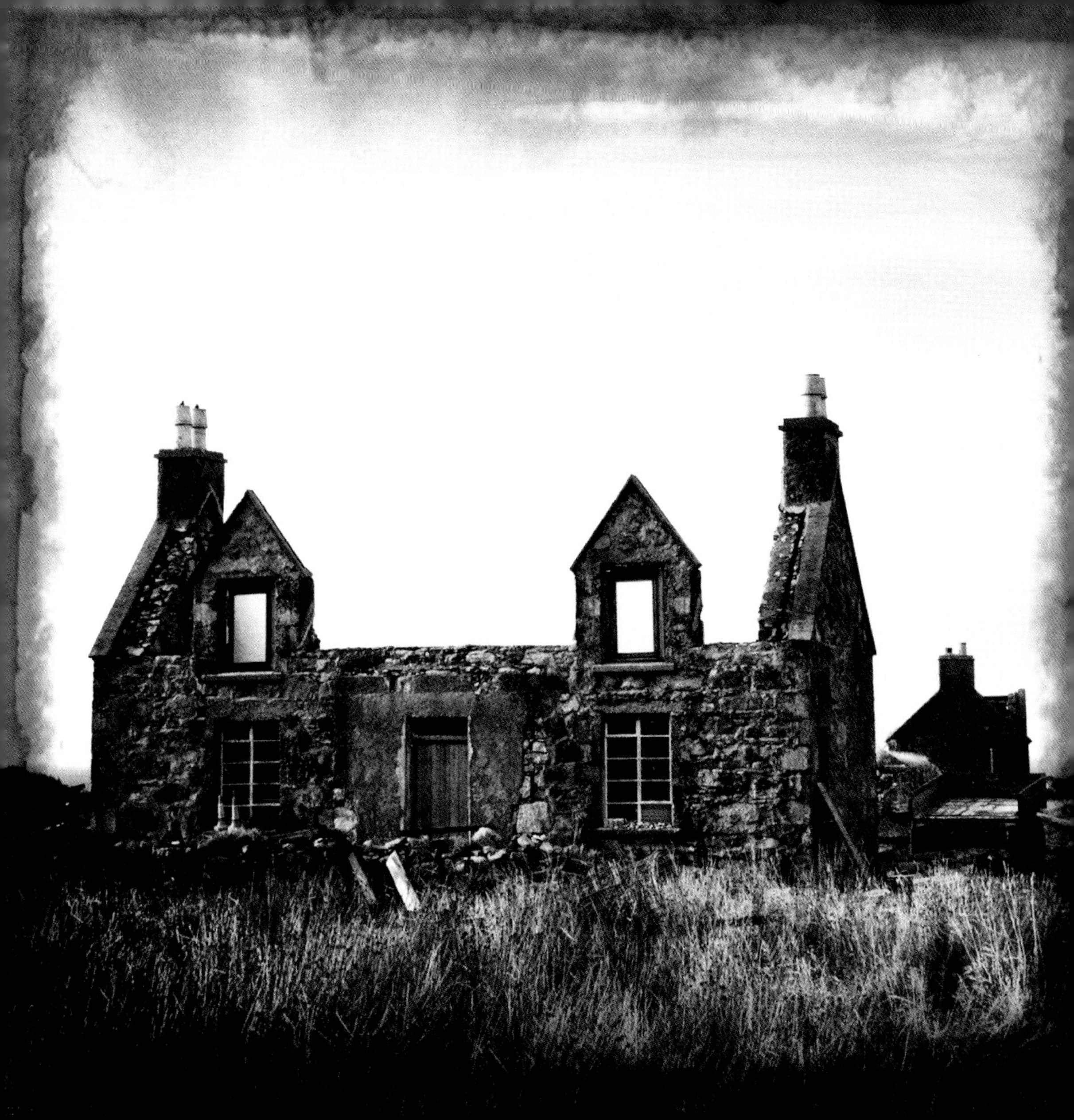

the jagged angles appeared through a gap in the October mist
the window glass solemn in its sombre distant reflection
and in the upper hidden crevices of an eastern wall
the blackbirds bickered and sang
channeling childhood arguments
chanting fireside fairy stories
frenetic and fabulously formed in the newly excavated trumpets
of the four cardinal chimneys
circumnavigating and redefining domesticity
forged in the fumes, flickers and fantasy
of paraffin

no anticipation
of the advance of electricity
a simple testament
a challenge
to join the dots and make connection
through genealogical snakes
and ladders
a series of systematic charismatic lineage games
traced in the memories, scratches and fingerprints on the window panes of life
demonstrably literate noughts and crosses
on a fading census
deconstructed
to tell the story
of the house of names

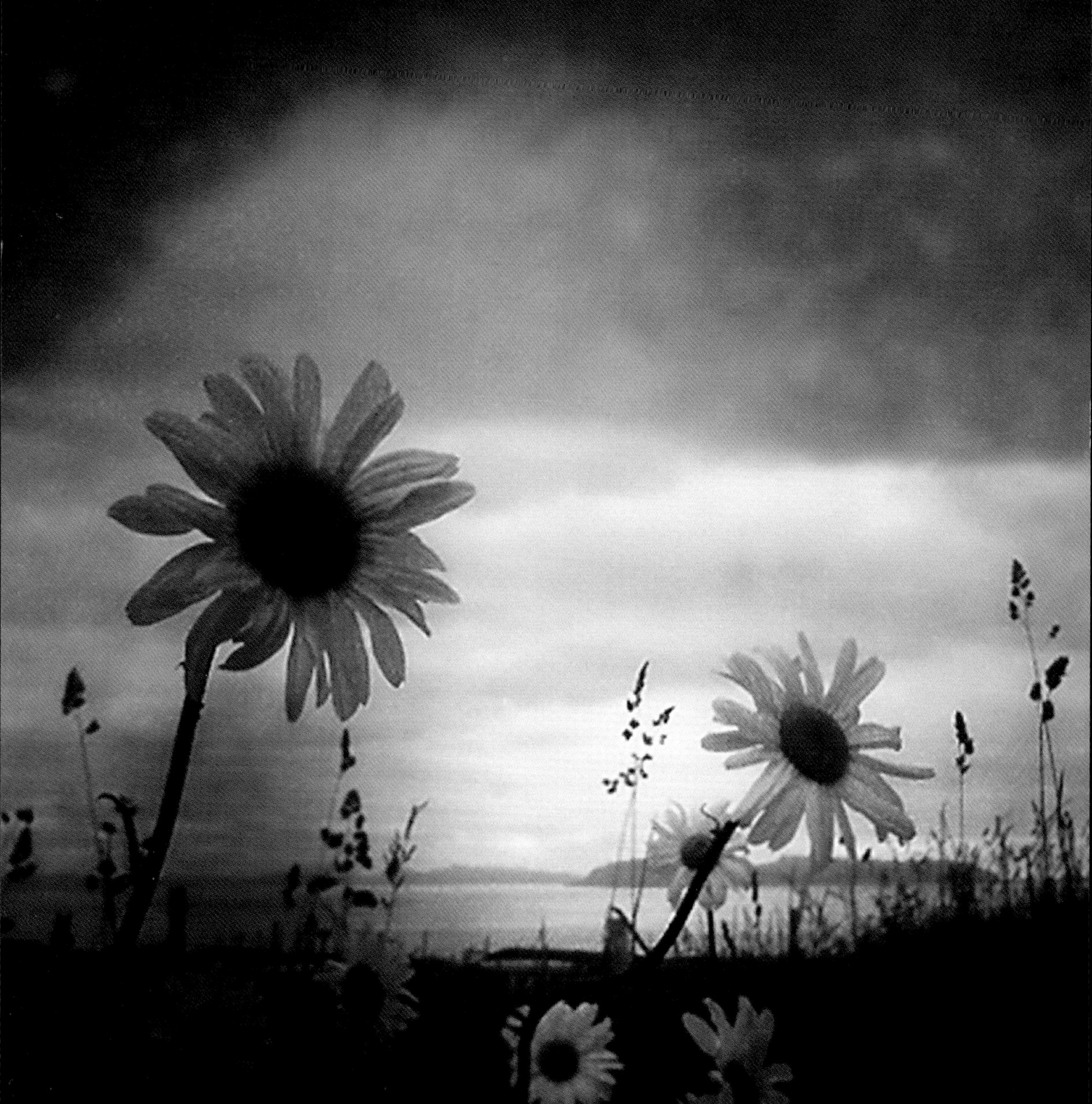

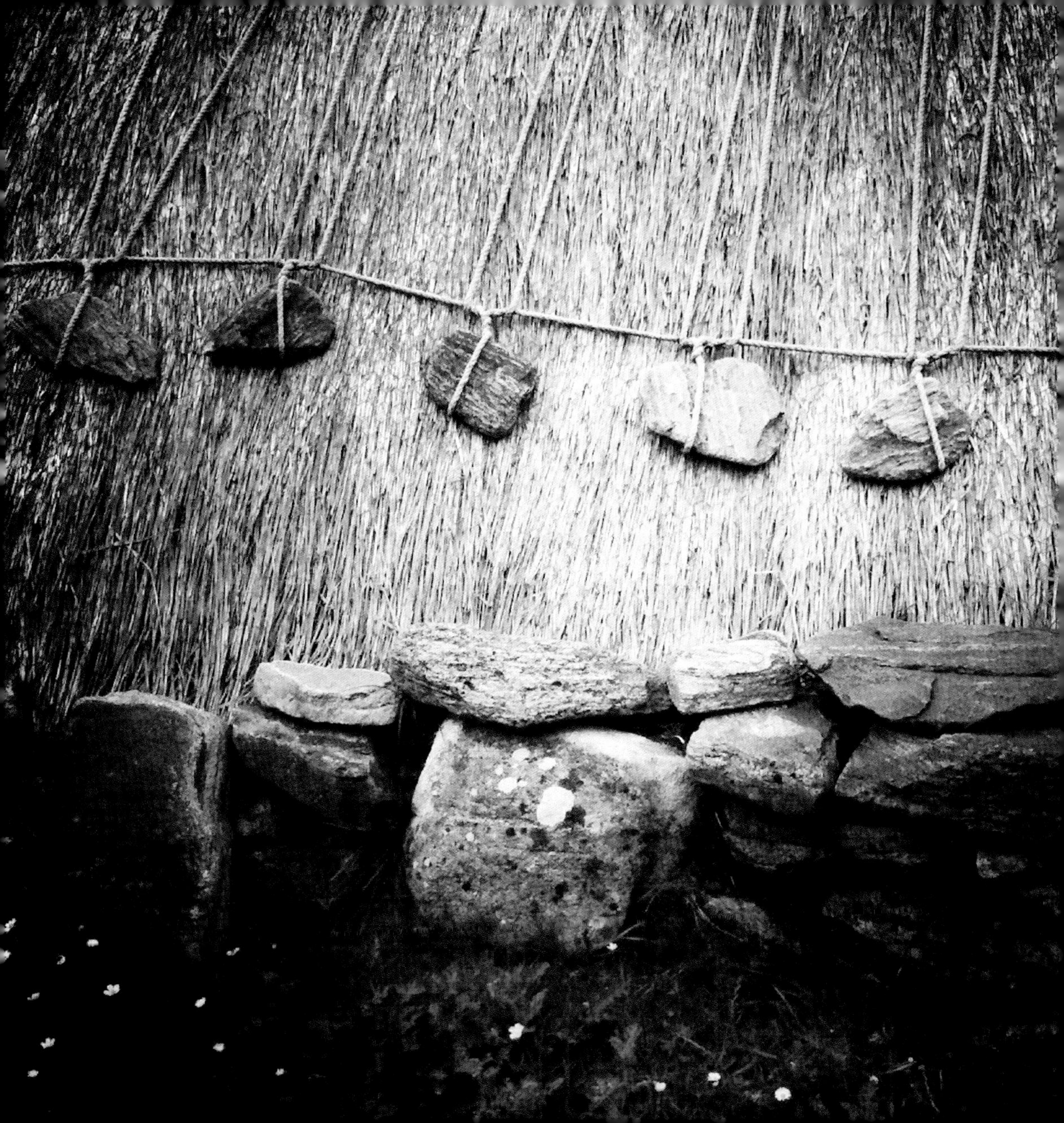

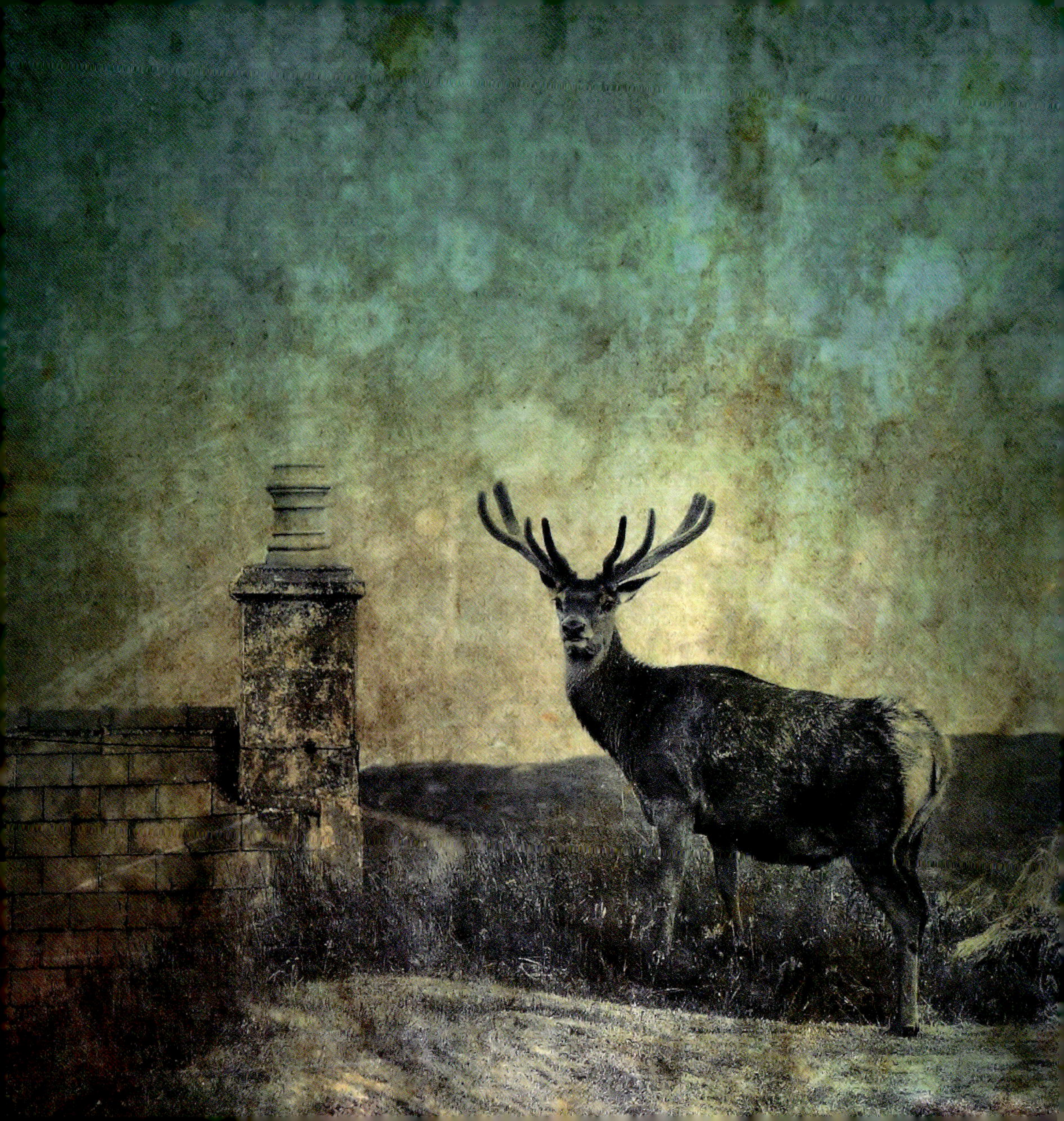

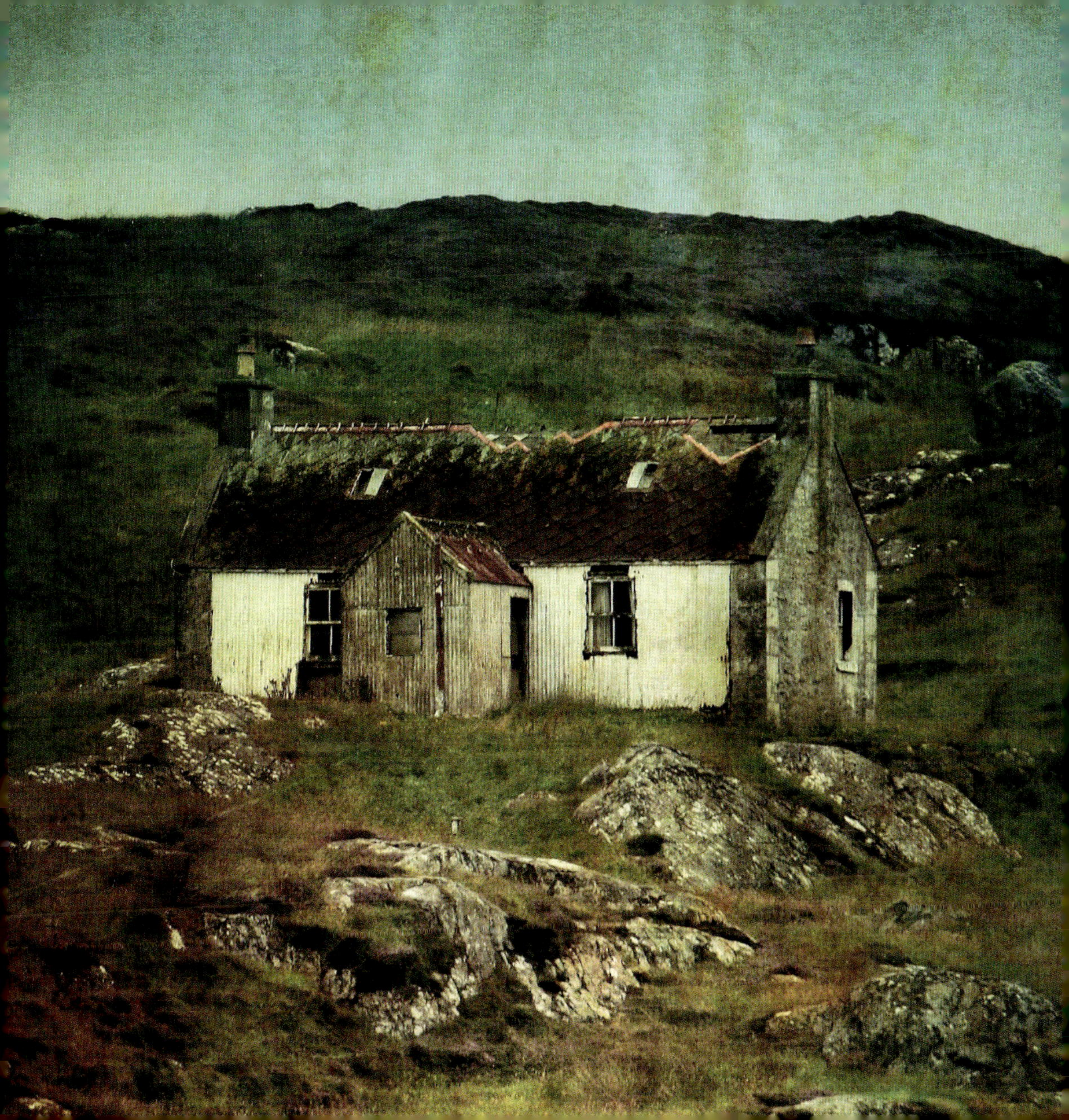

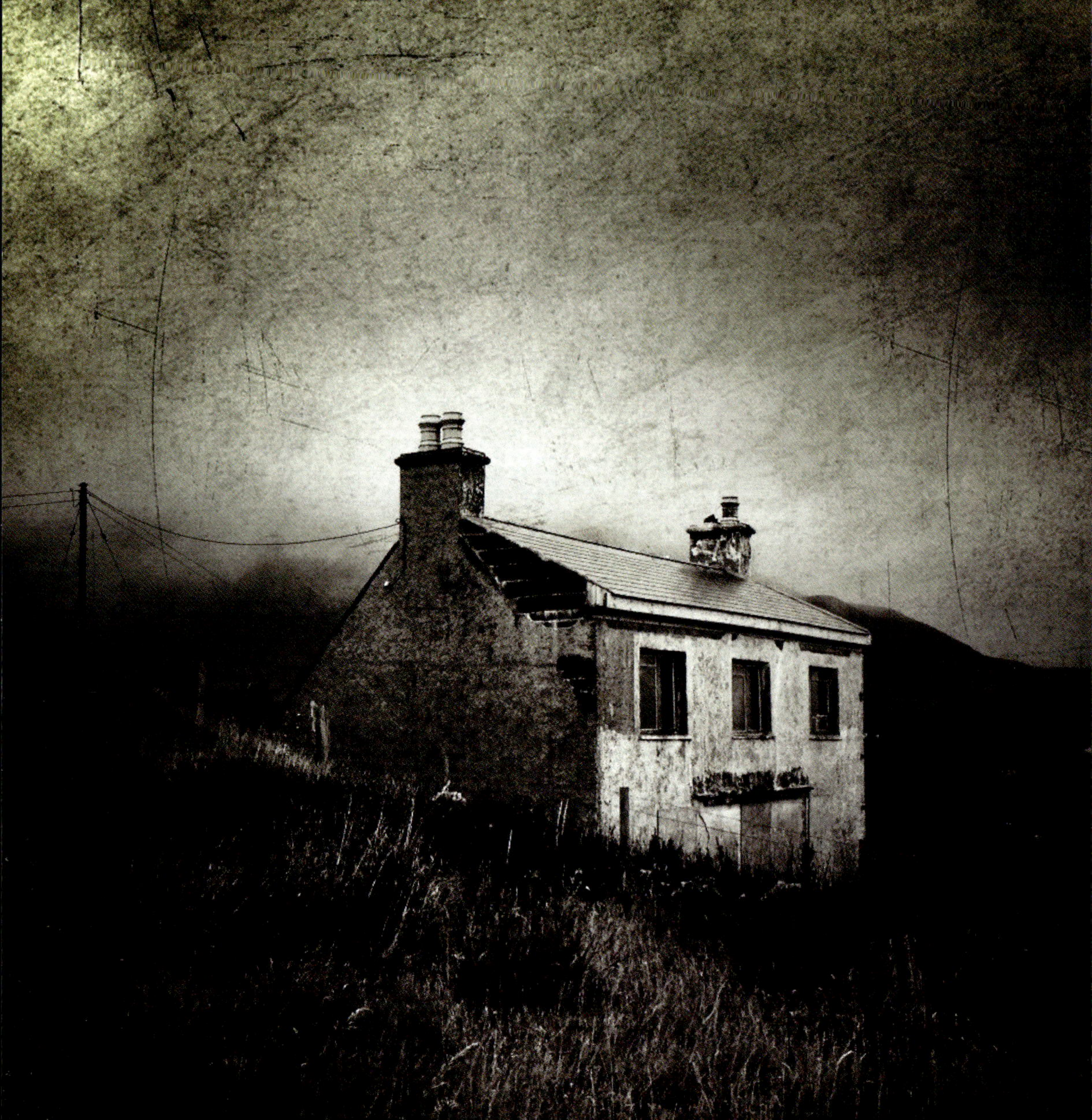

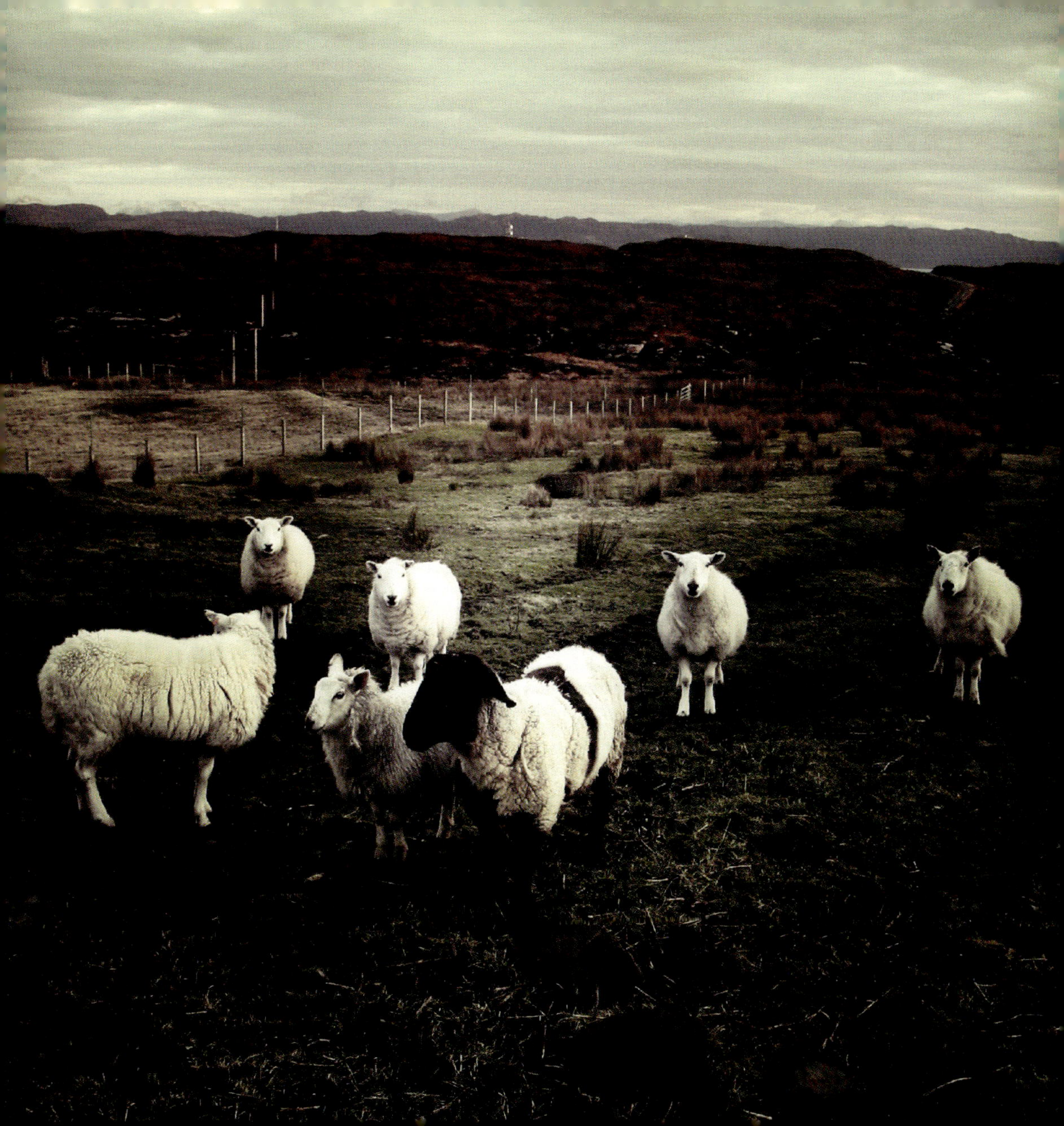

is there romance in ruin?

that summer,
driving around the island
singing ship to shore
an idiosyncratic beat from Luxembourg
crackling and cantankerous
from the speaker
in the creaky draughty
baler twined door

a temporarily isolated containment
no thought of wider engagement
in fashion
or future
or tension
or time

a world of spacemen
a world of travelling
twists and shouts from passengers
gratuitous and garrulous and grinding,
the road unravelling
blind
twisting, turning, winding
cassette tape reminiscences
forwarding, hesitating, rewinding

carried out
and carrying on
passing place memories
interrupt the song

some say that memories
are not for fools
regulations
they don't mean rules

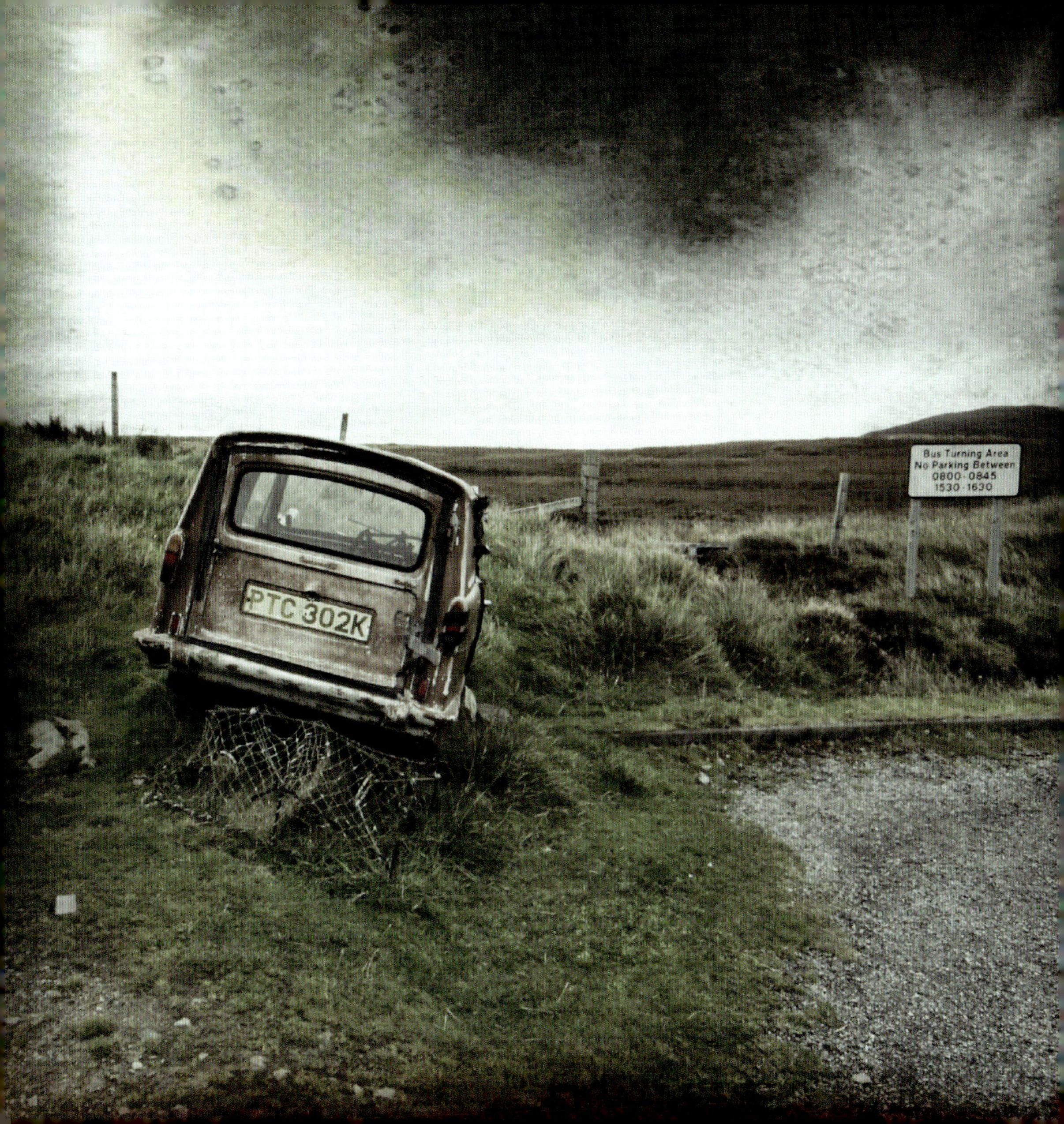
PTC 302K
Bus Turning Area
No Parking Between
0800-0845
1530-1630

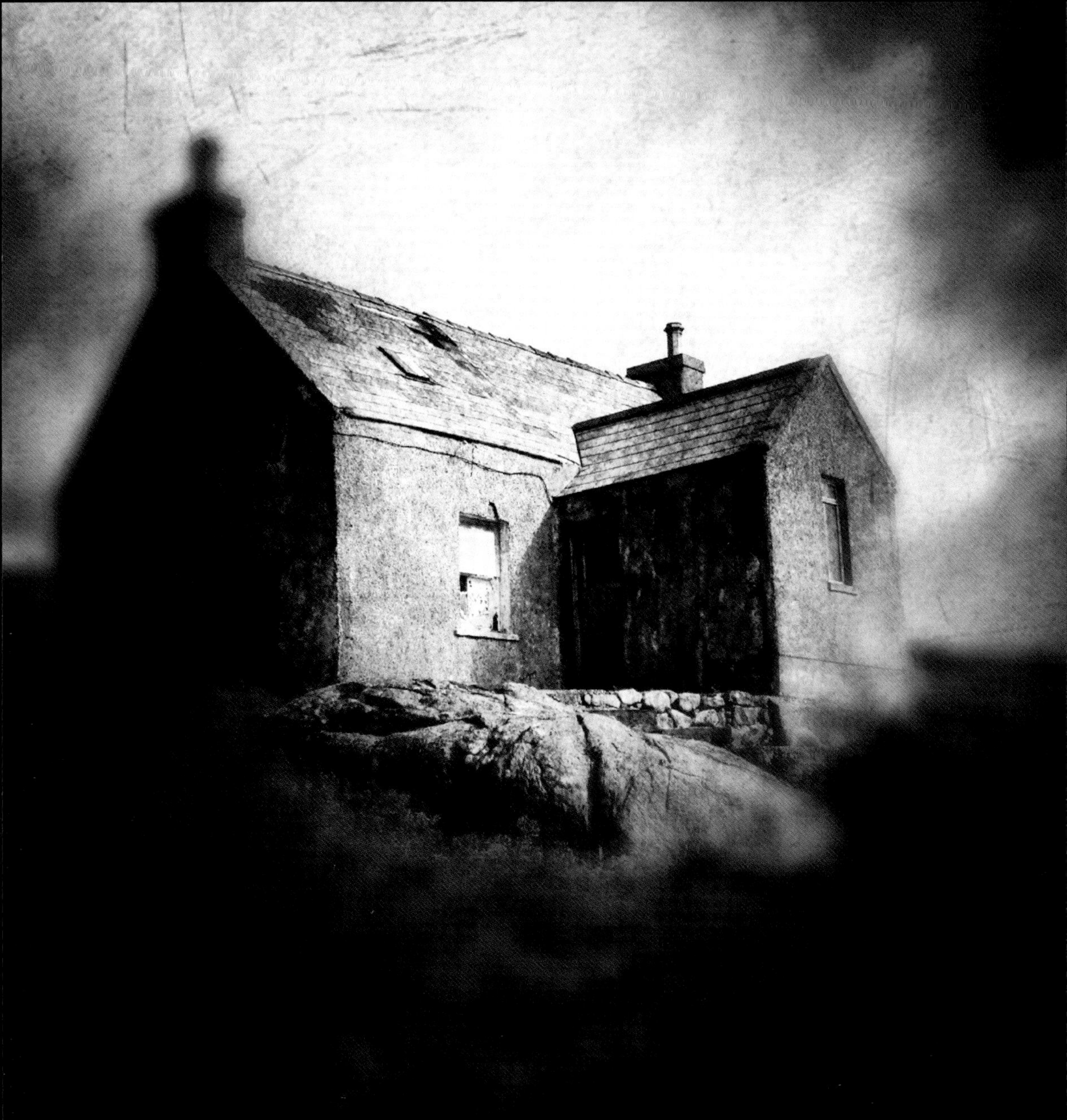

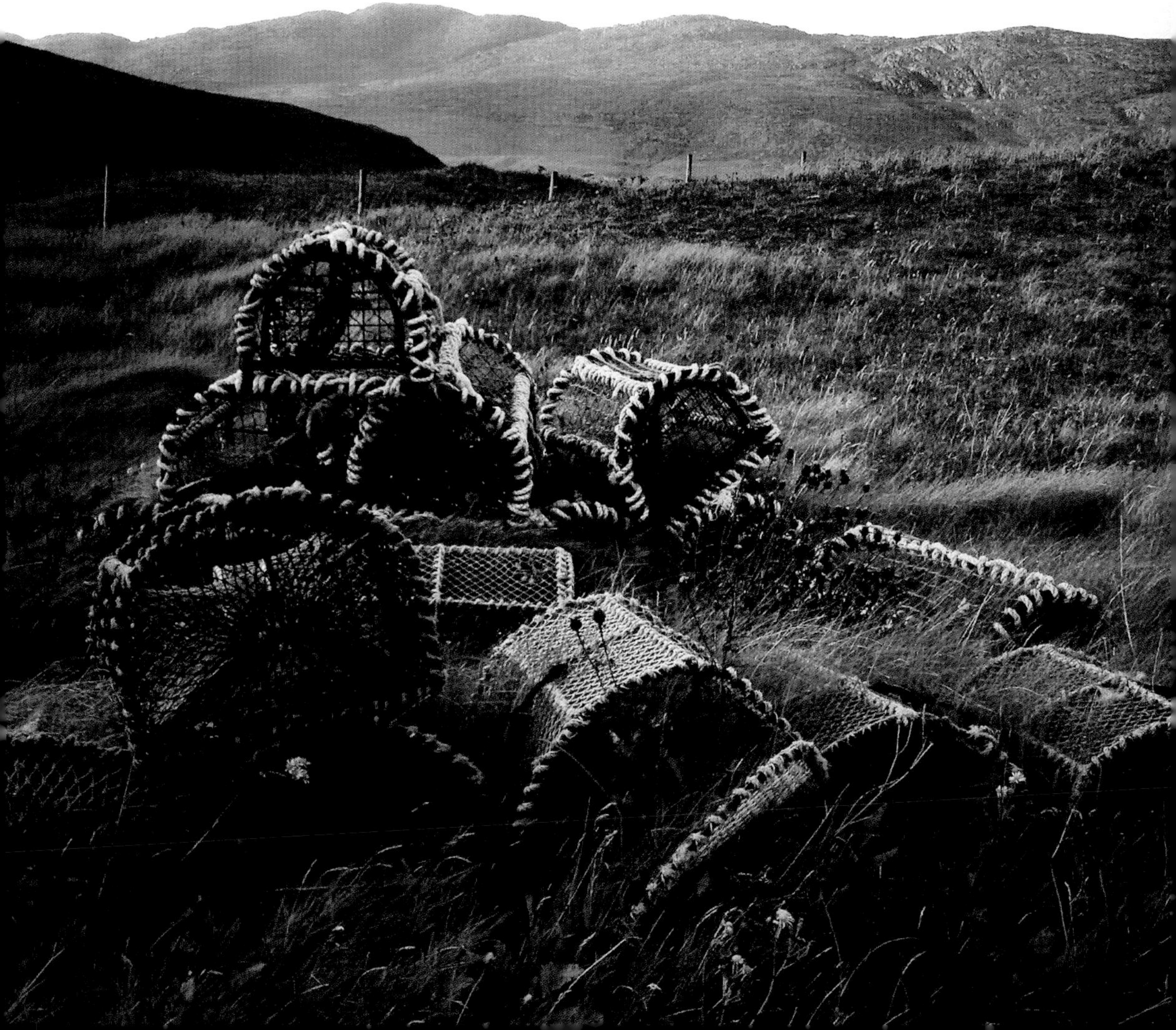

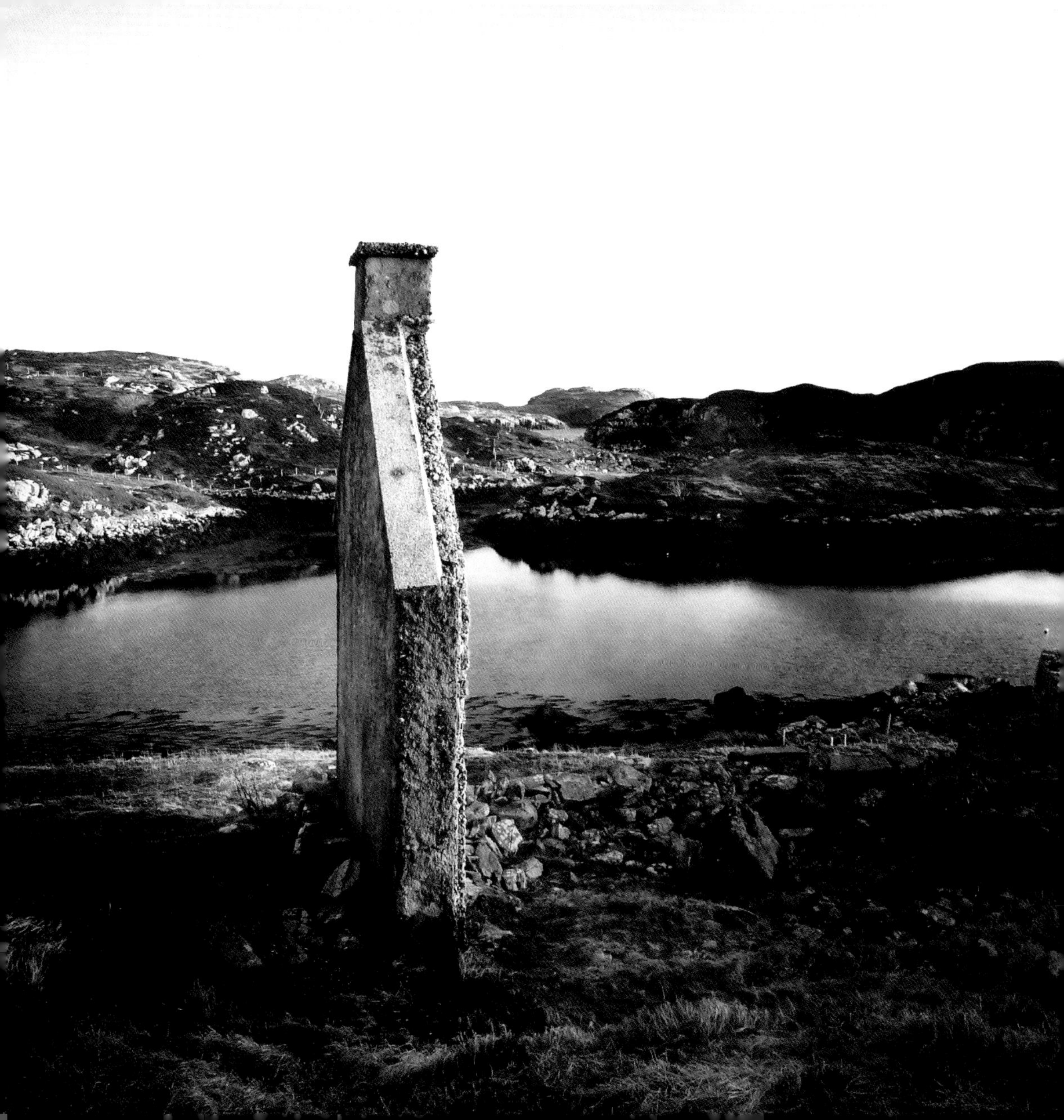

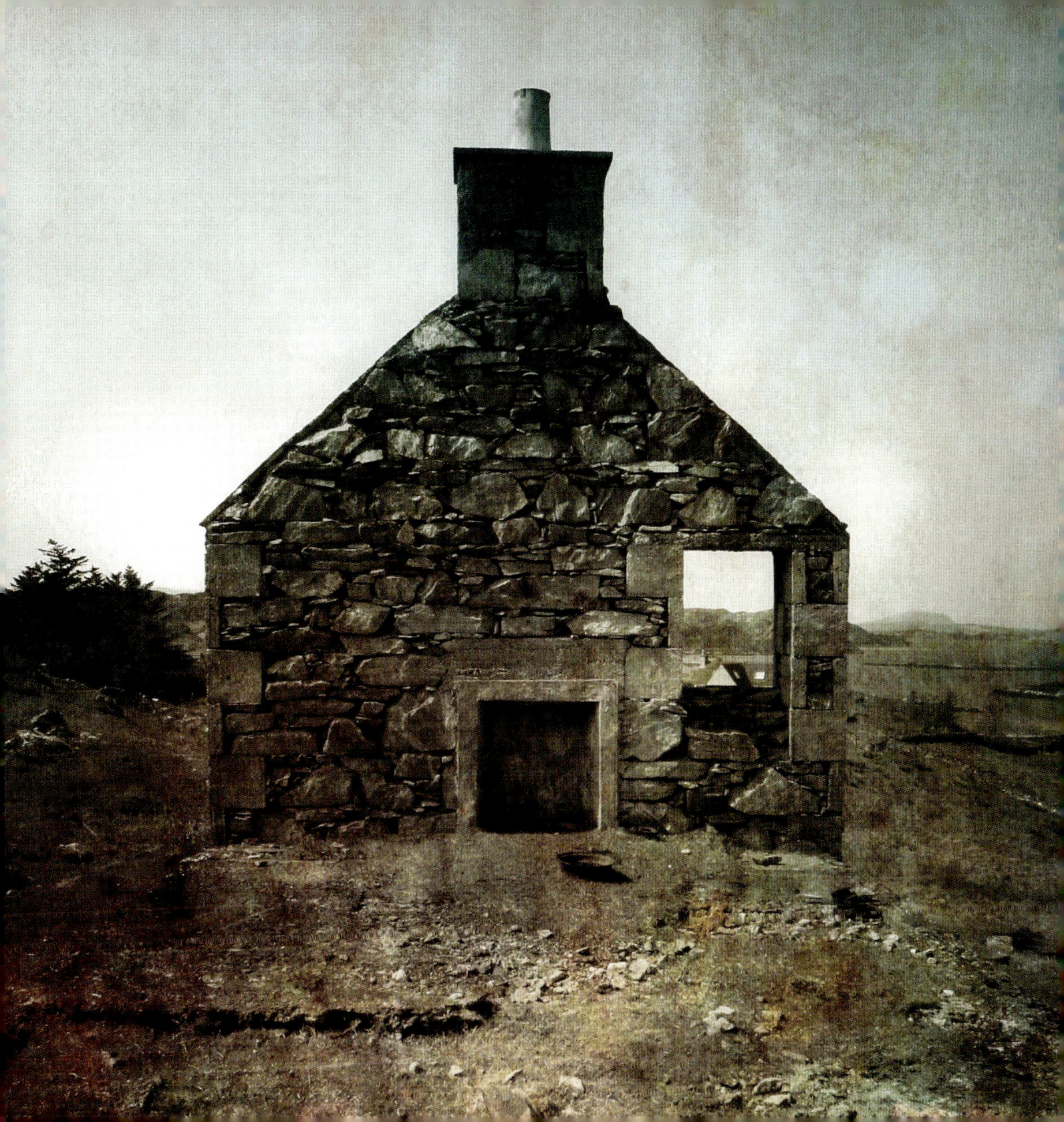

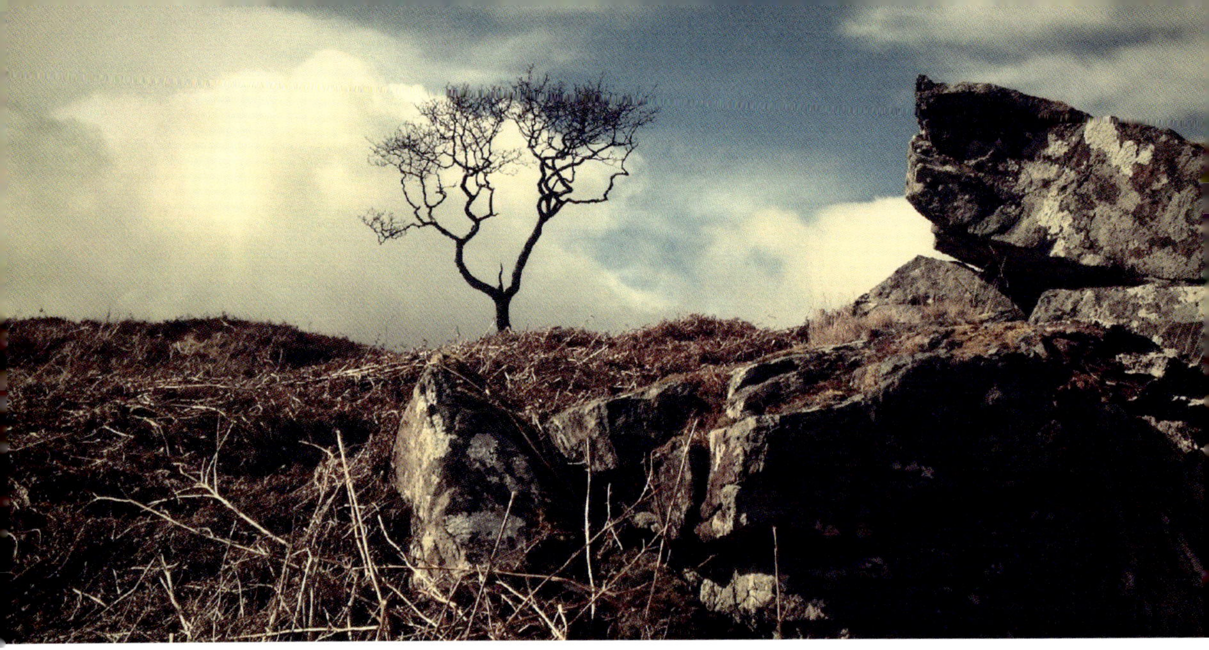

I suspect no-one knows
that this is a tree of life?

where ancestors meet to offer wisdom
to those who seek reunion
with memory

a genealogical oasis
full of laughter
experience
reassurance
routine

where all of the steps of the dance
can be remembered and replayed
in glowing tribute
to the re-accumulation of the stepping stones
of wisdom

nursery rhymes are celebrated
misplaced childhoods returned
the reunited argue
and smile

and if you visit,
take heed of the opportunity
to rekindle and enjoy the friendly advice
and deliverance
and certainty
of reconnected
time

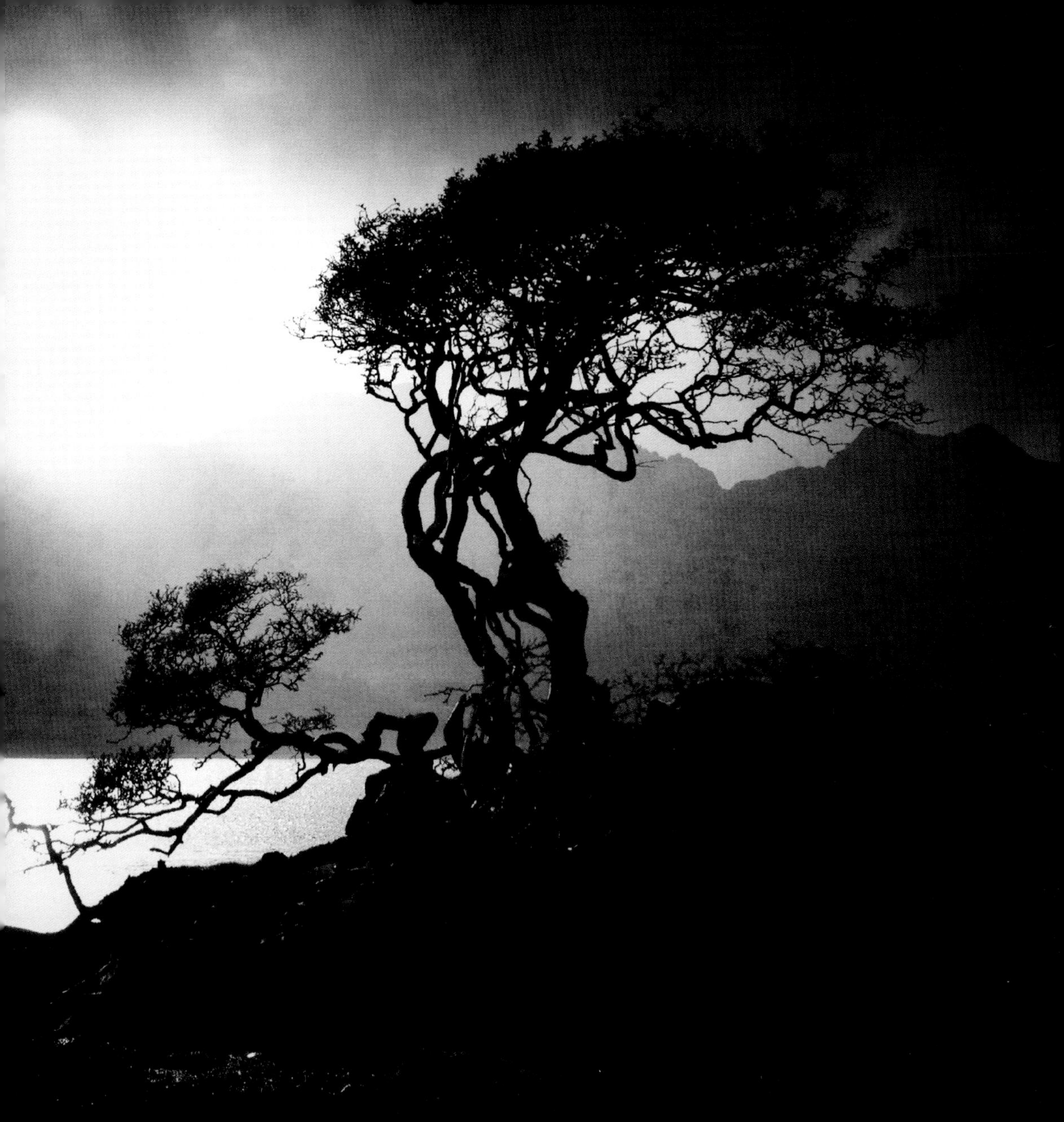

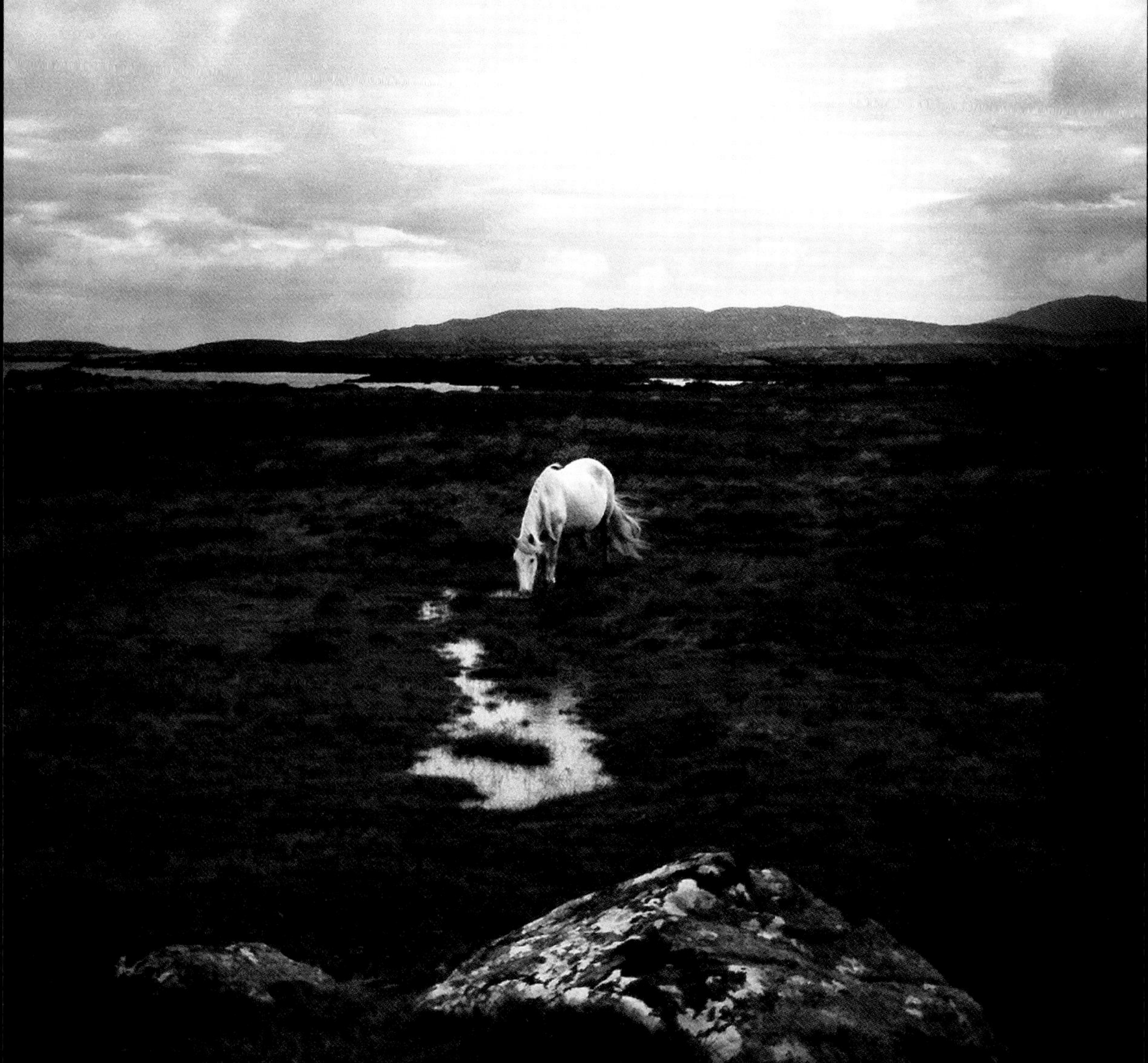

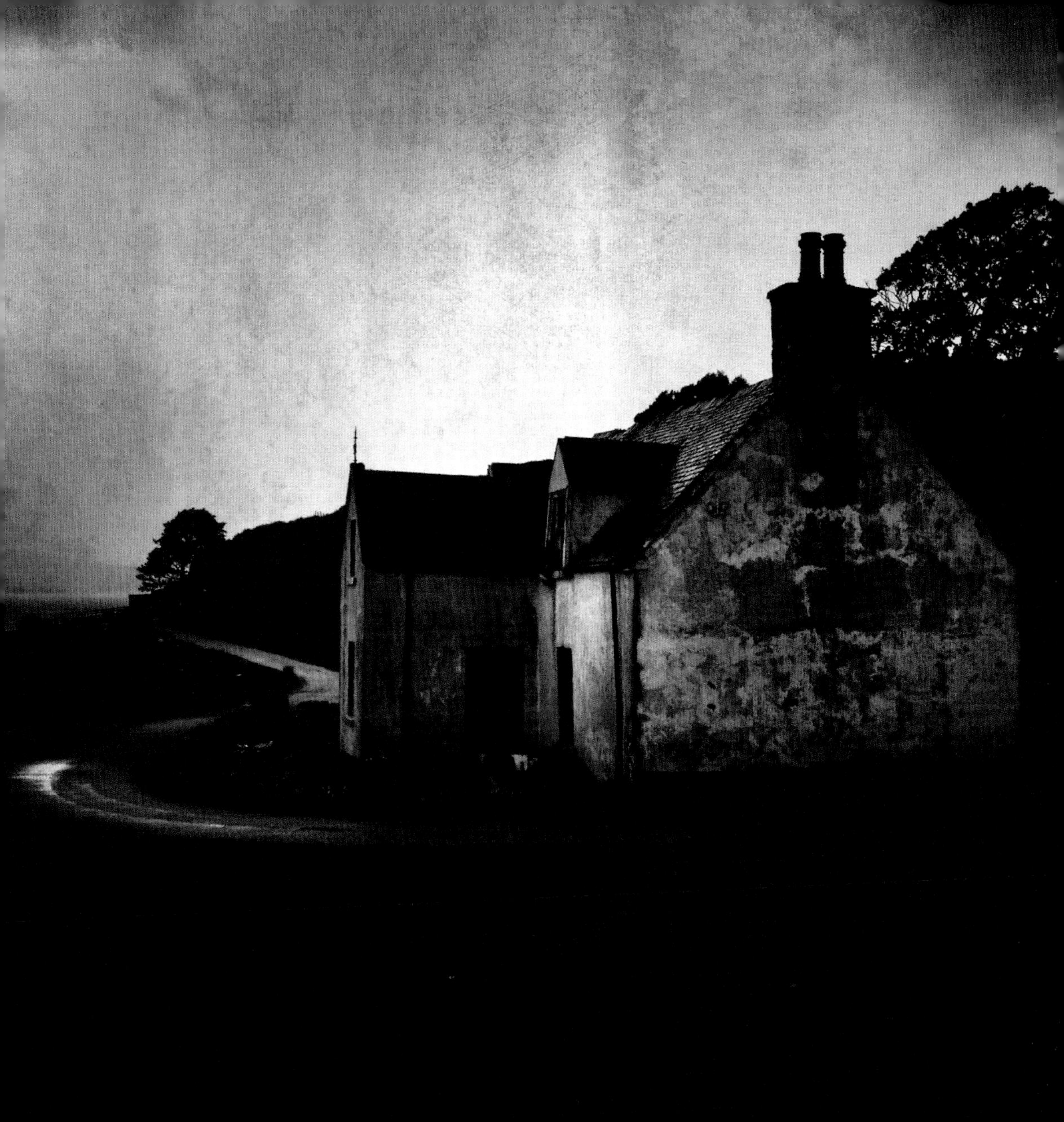

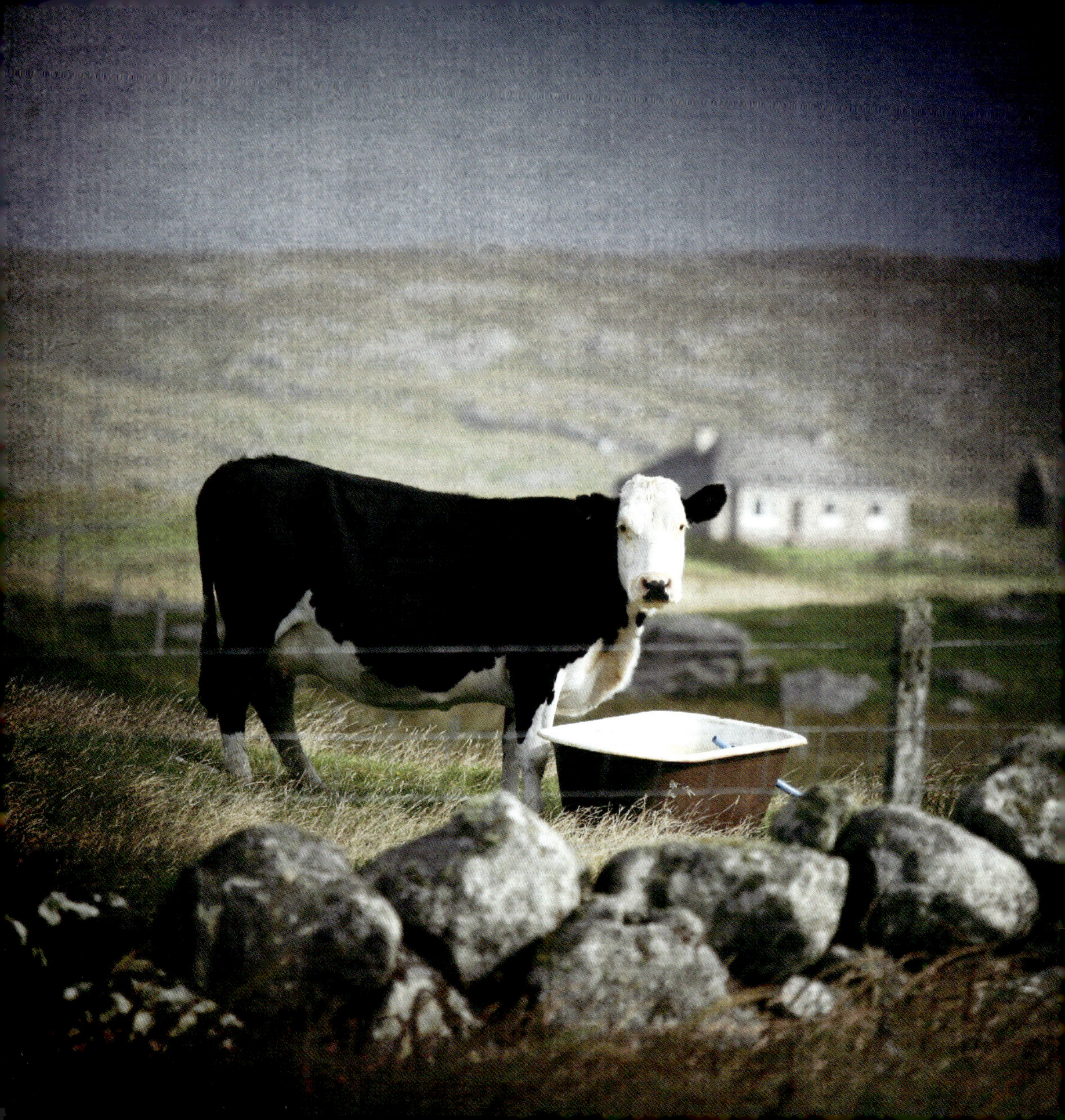

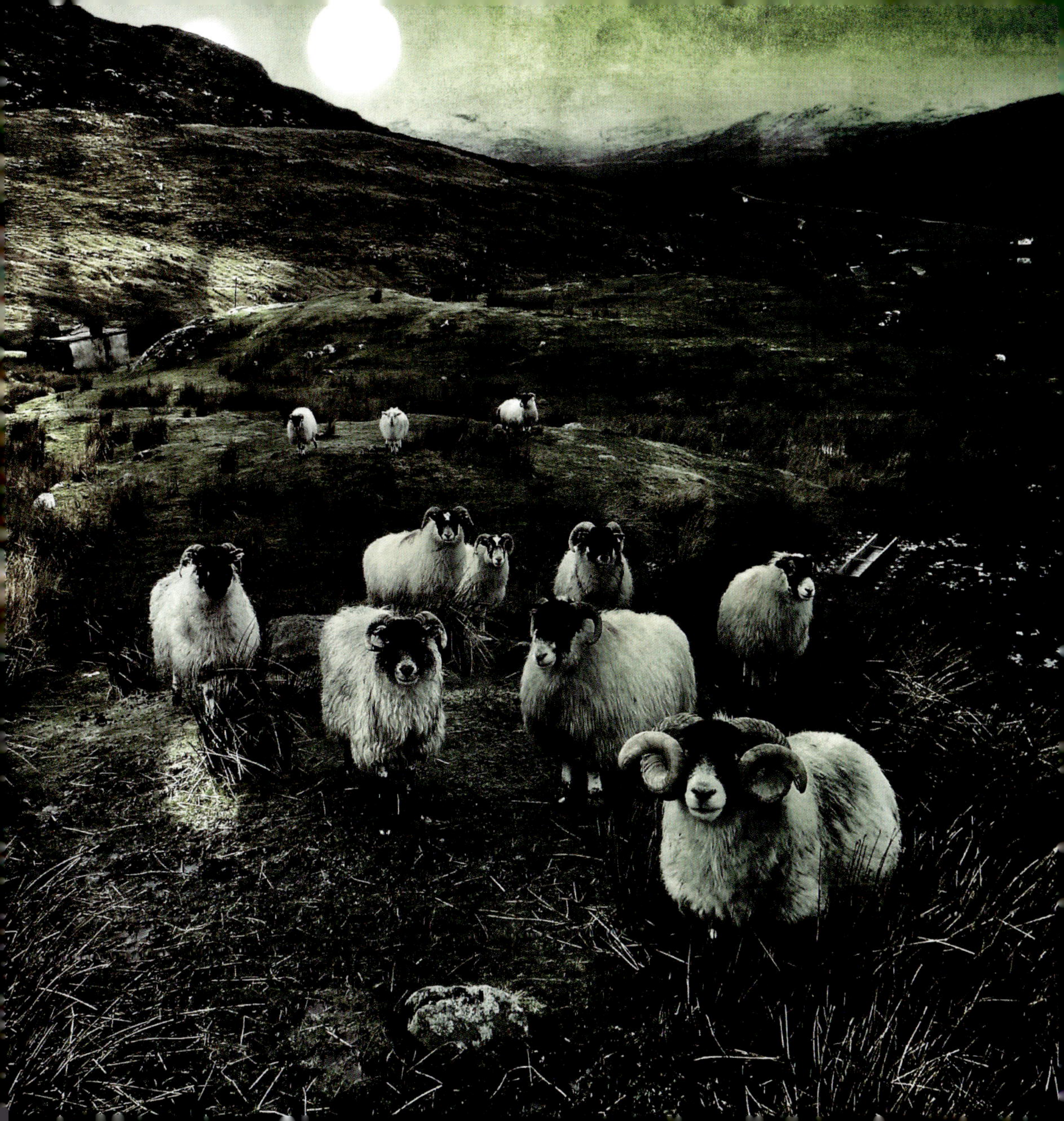

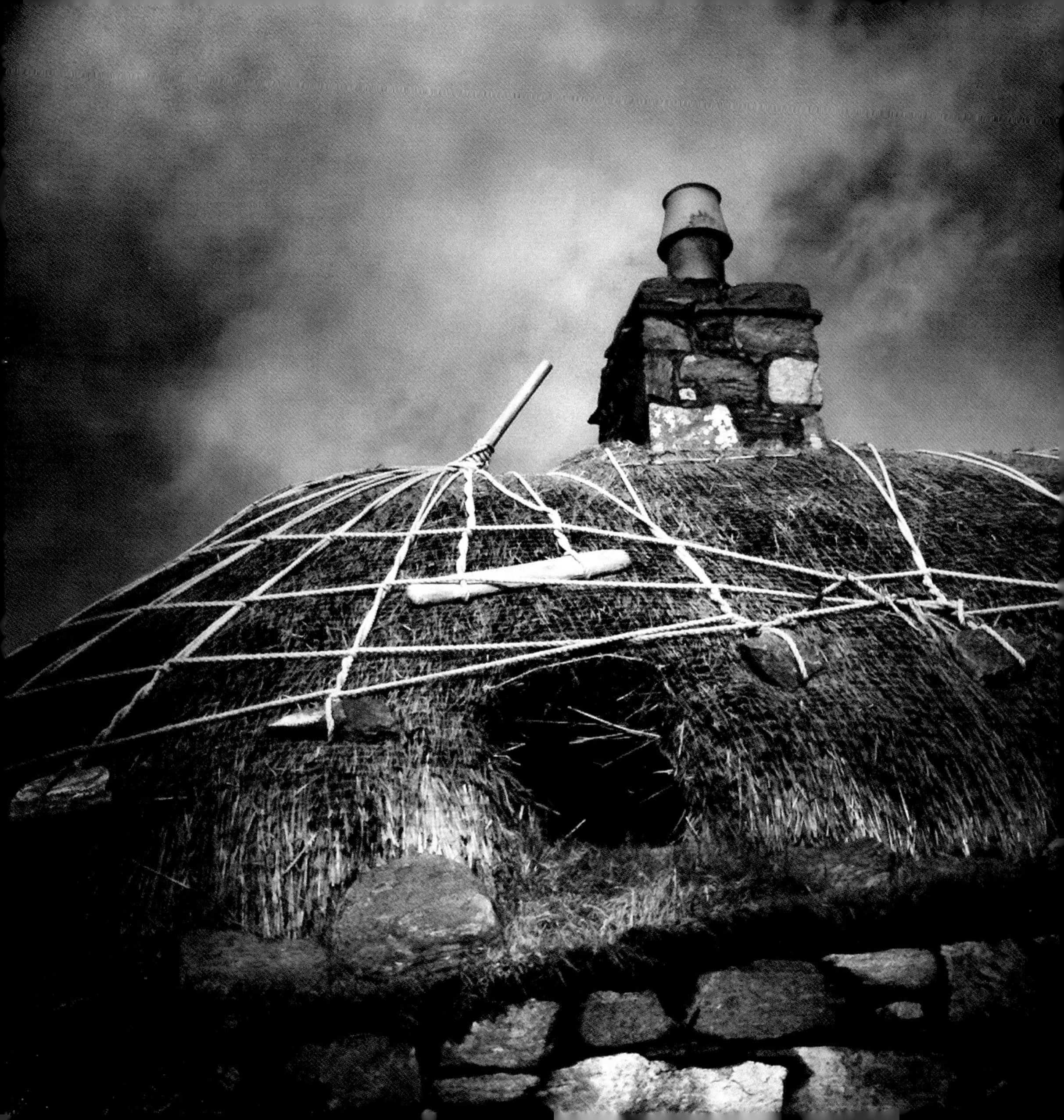

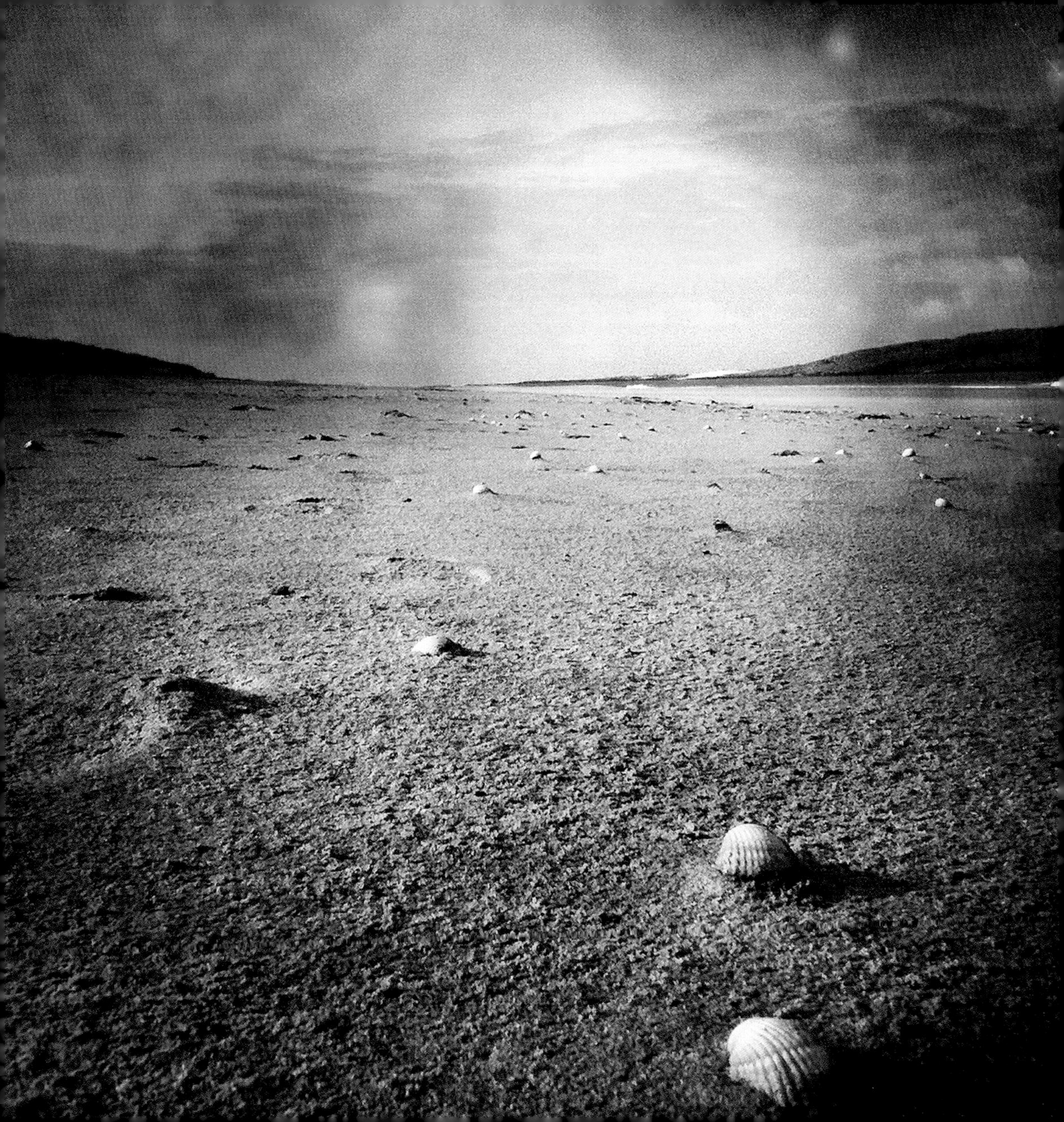

is there romance in ruin?

in the summer
life returns
to this superficially broken home
a new transhumance cycle brings curiosity to the ribbed pastures
swallows play games of dare
with the skeletoned bones
and the Japanese backpackers devour the carcass of packaged emotions
that mask and wallpaper over
the question of nuance and dexterity in culture
identity and verse
ideas rewind, reiterate and reverse
in a dichotomy of persuasively random appraisal

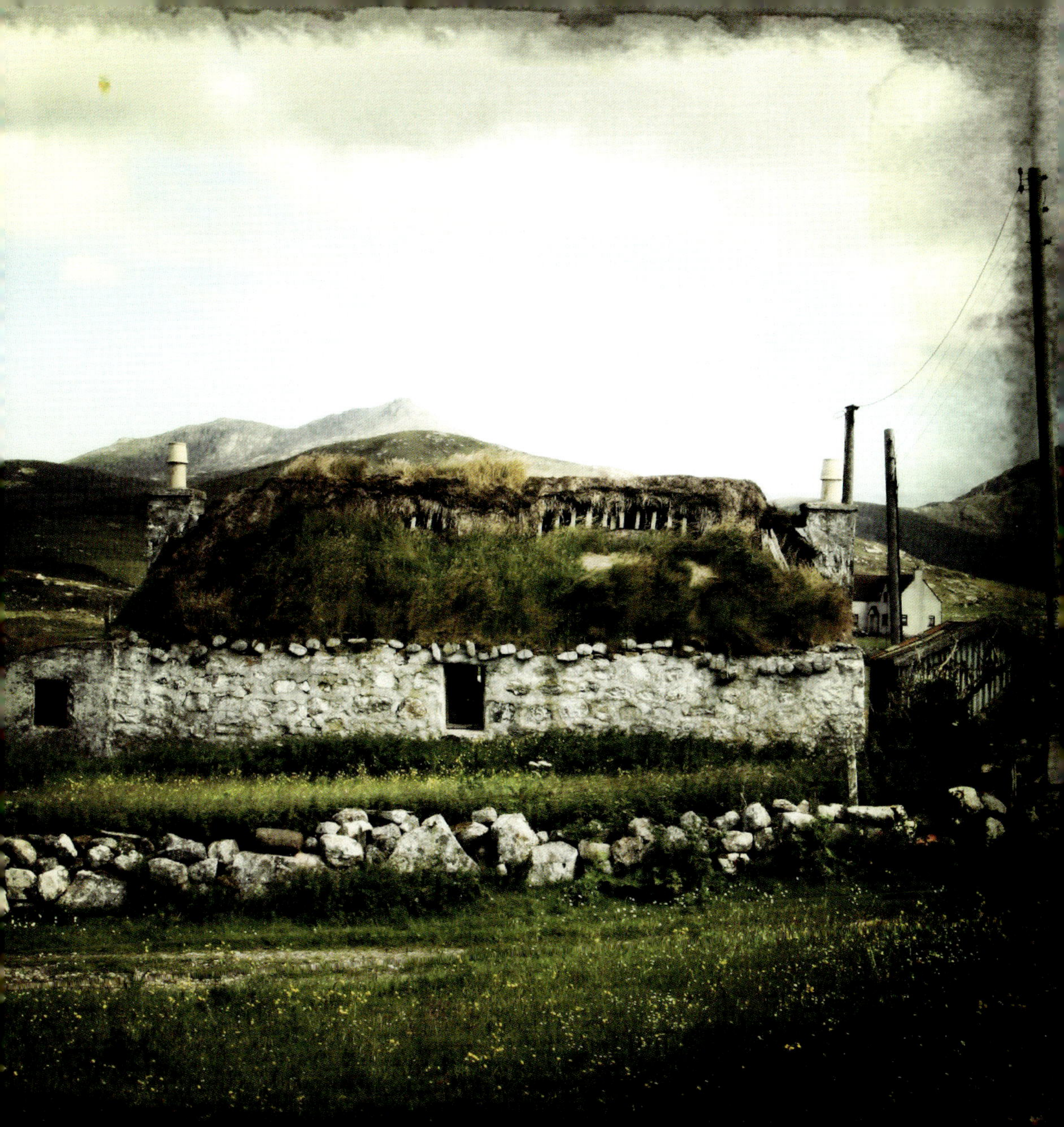

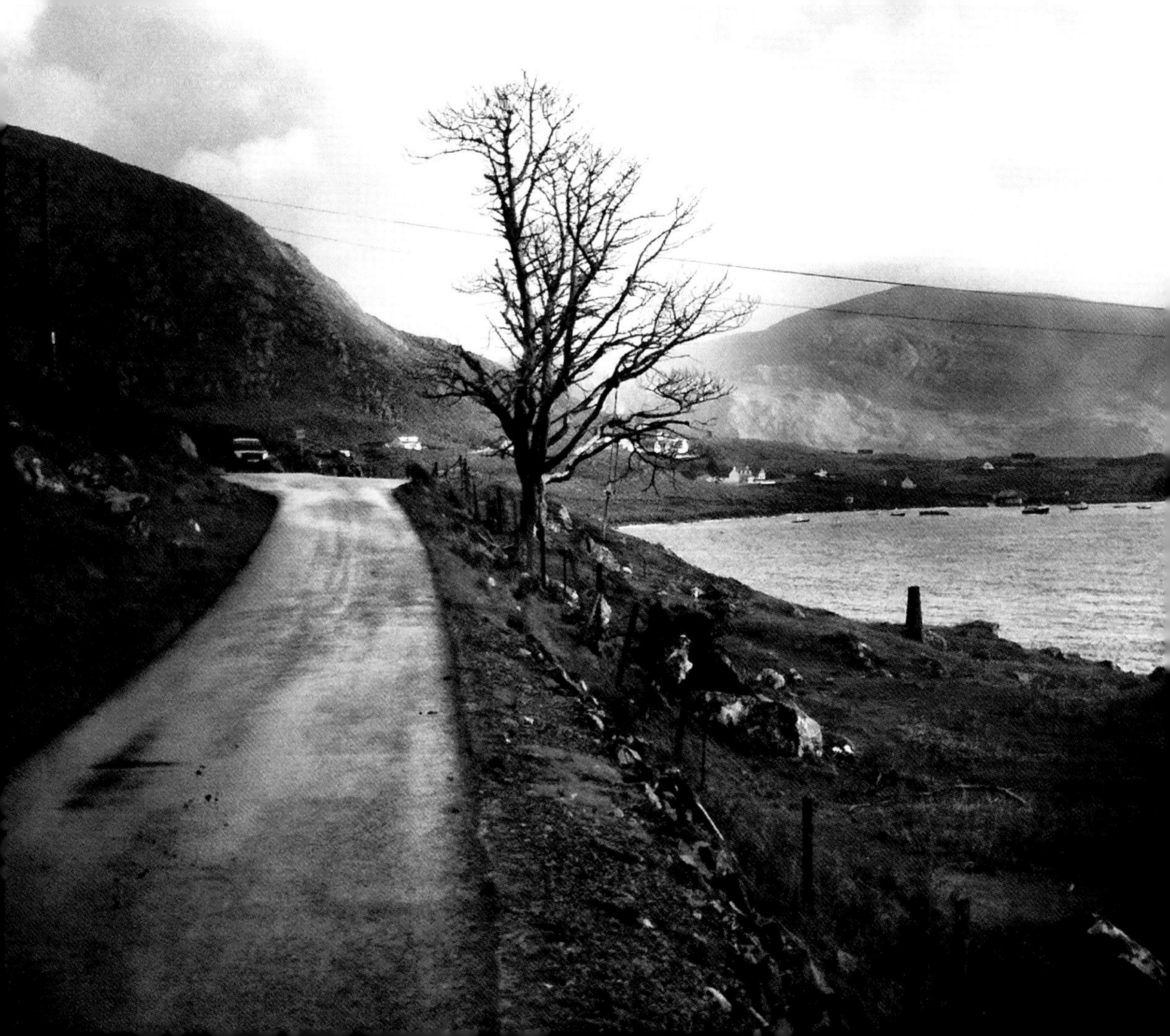

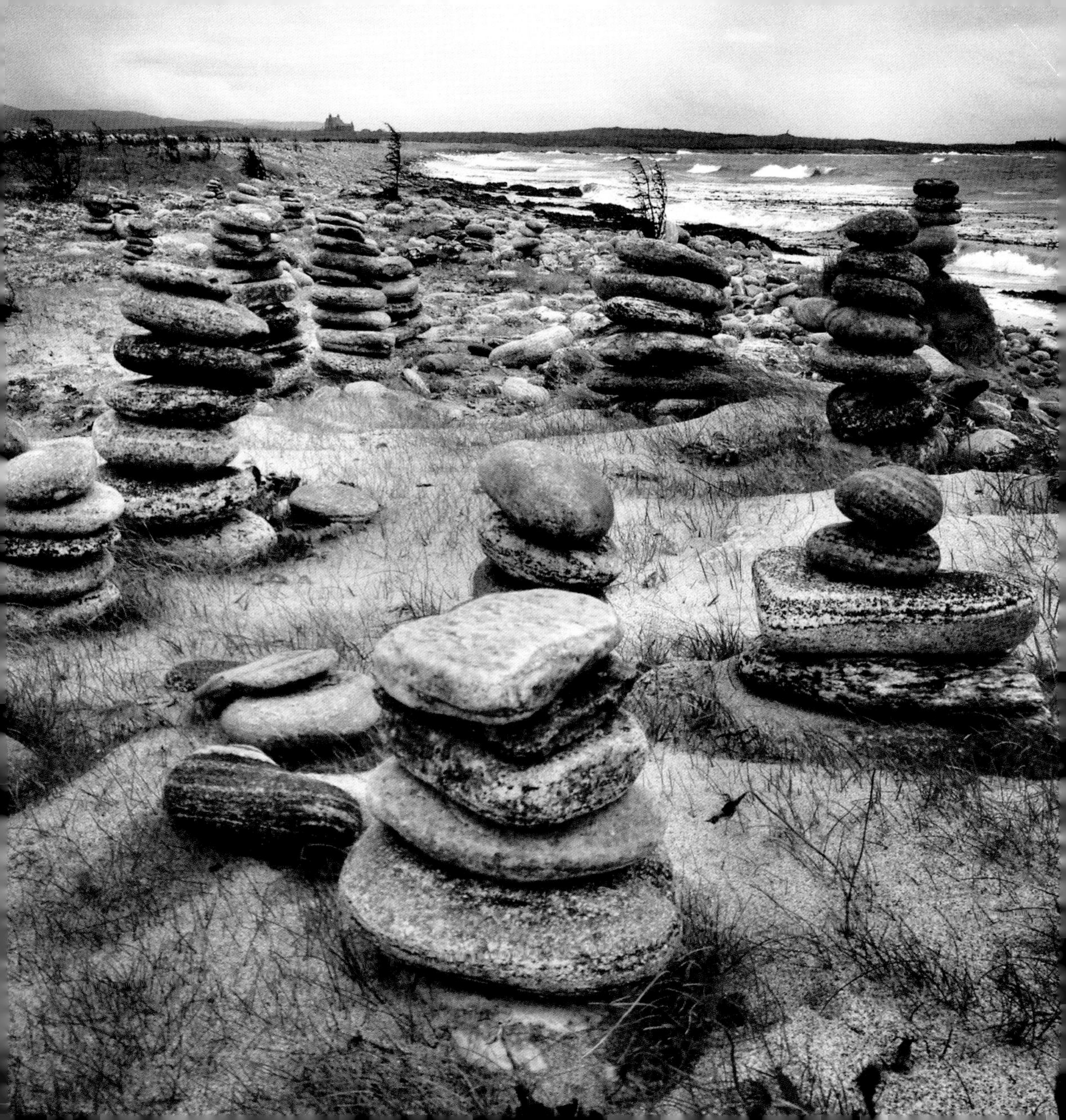

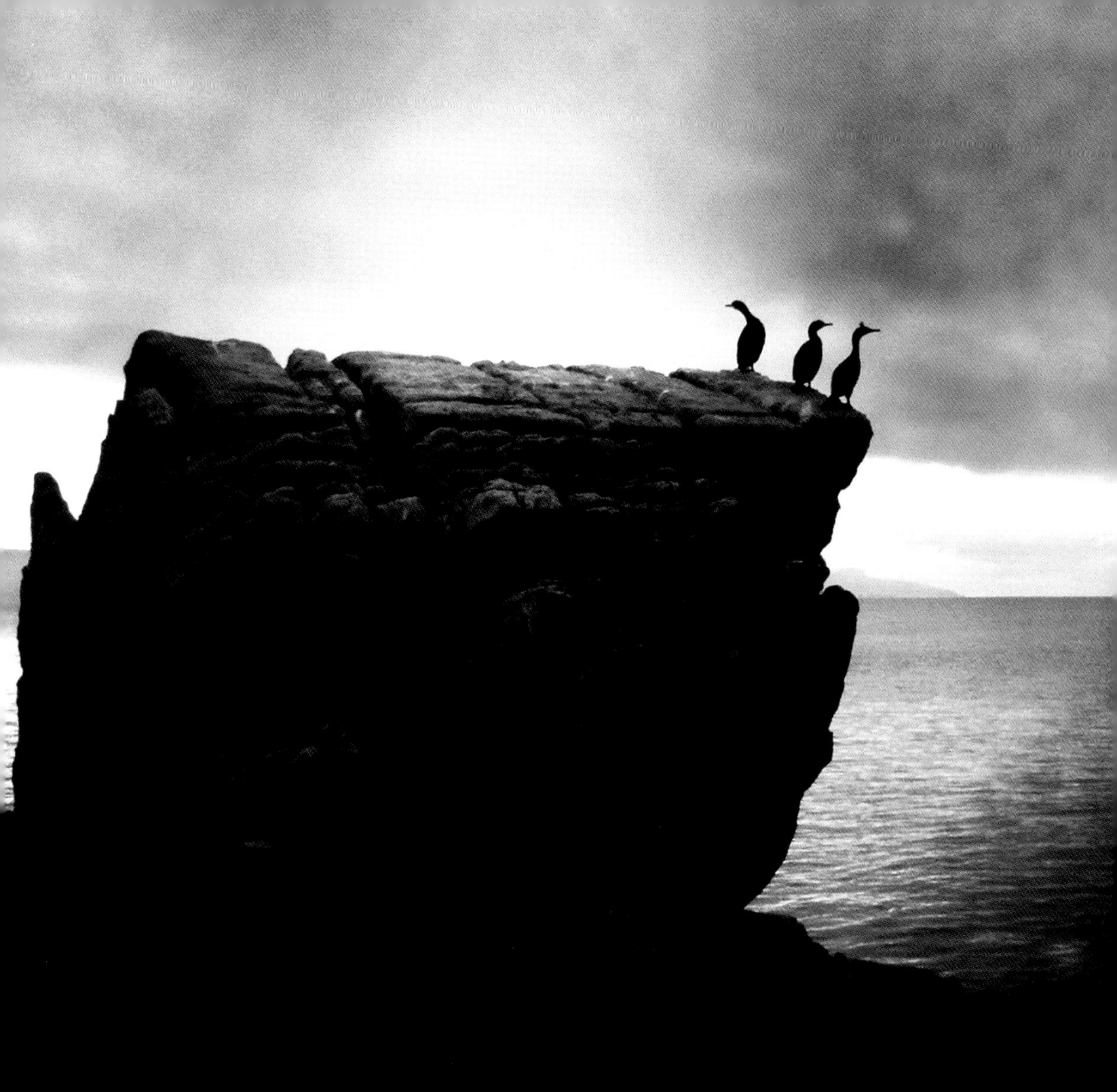

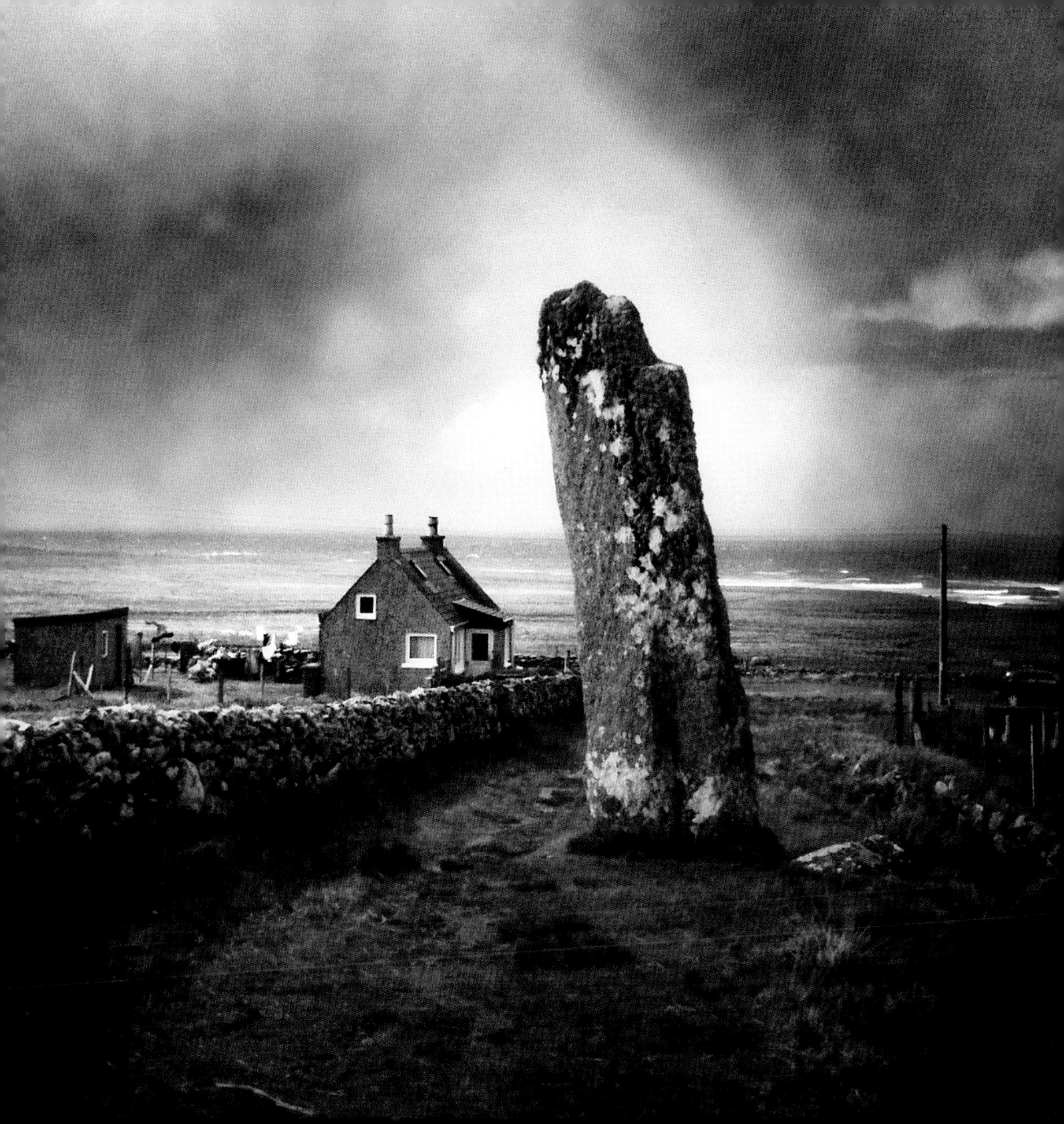

protecting the grave of the eagle
the little mountain ash
remains resolute
against the approaching storms of indifference
guarding the abandoned pasture
with a fiery autumnal intent

damping the enthusiasm of incantation and spell
securing the site of the guardian's well

resistant
resolutely persistent
repelling the irritant gesture
of the wild land speculator

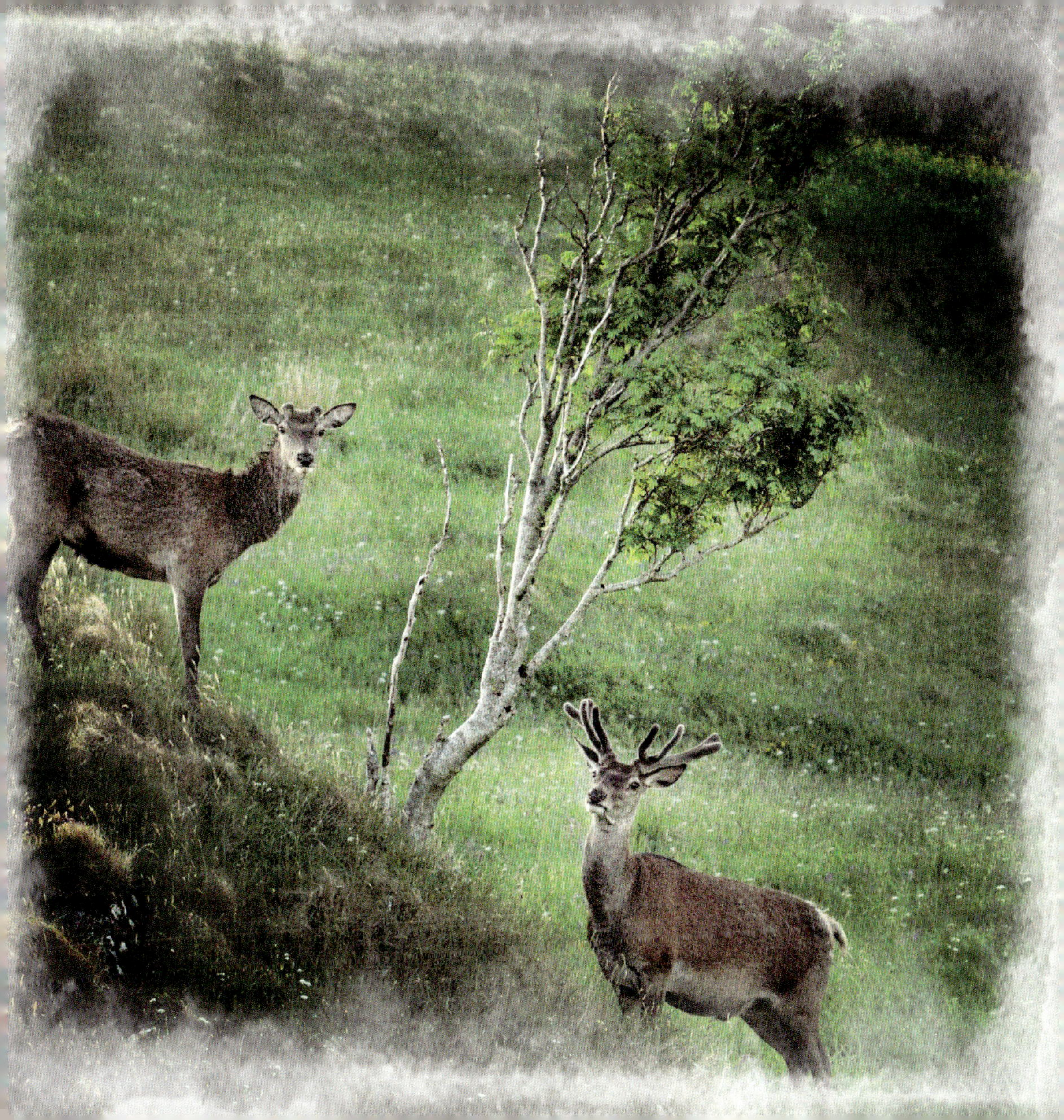

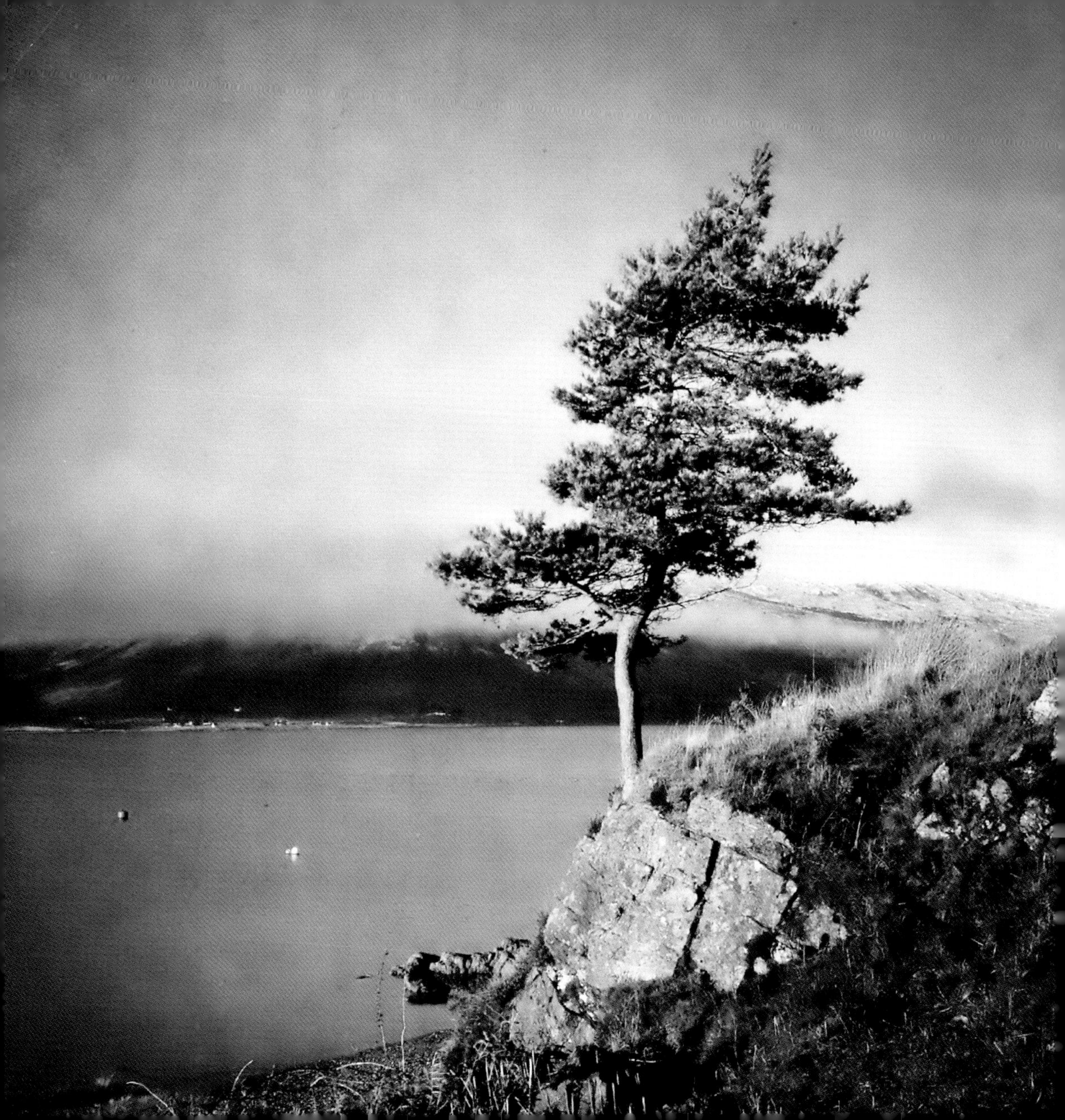

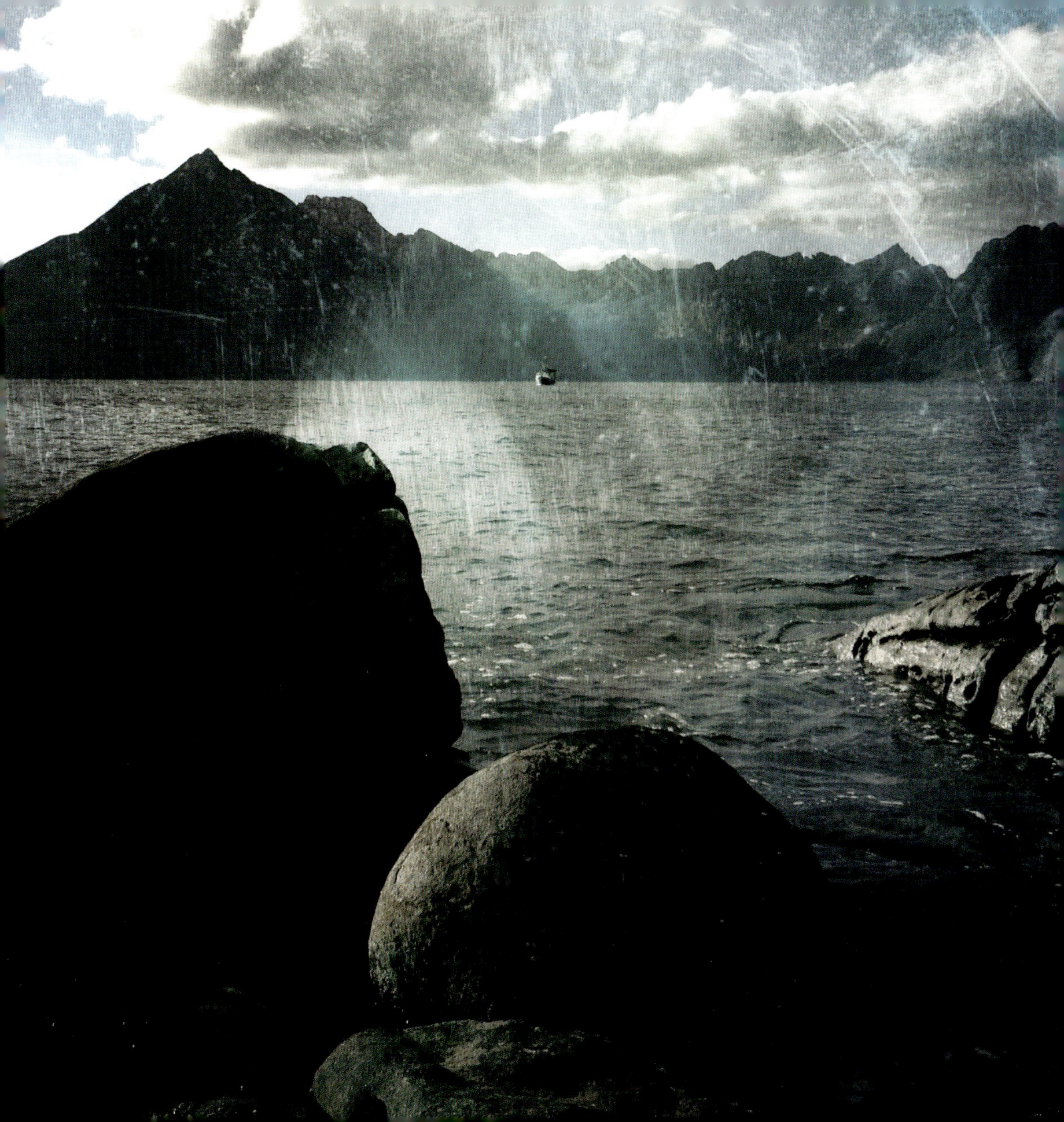

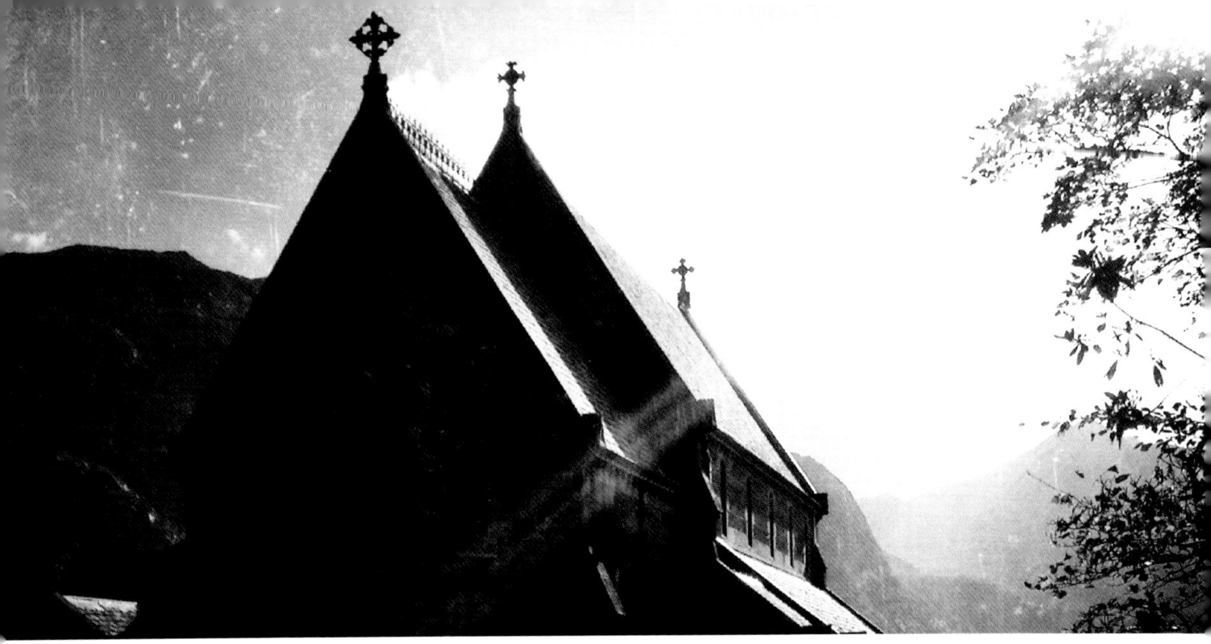

if you listen
you might just hear the bell
its rhyme benevolent
sympathetic to the ivy mask
cloaking the fabric in an emotional virtuous entanglement
of mystical song
reinforcing in costume
the procession and pomp
of a time long gone

the little chapel
saintly and tenaciously
retaining within its foundation walls
the relics and commandments
of its mission
in denial of the secular intermission
if you listen you might just hear the choir
in the cradle of saint anne de l'espoir

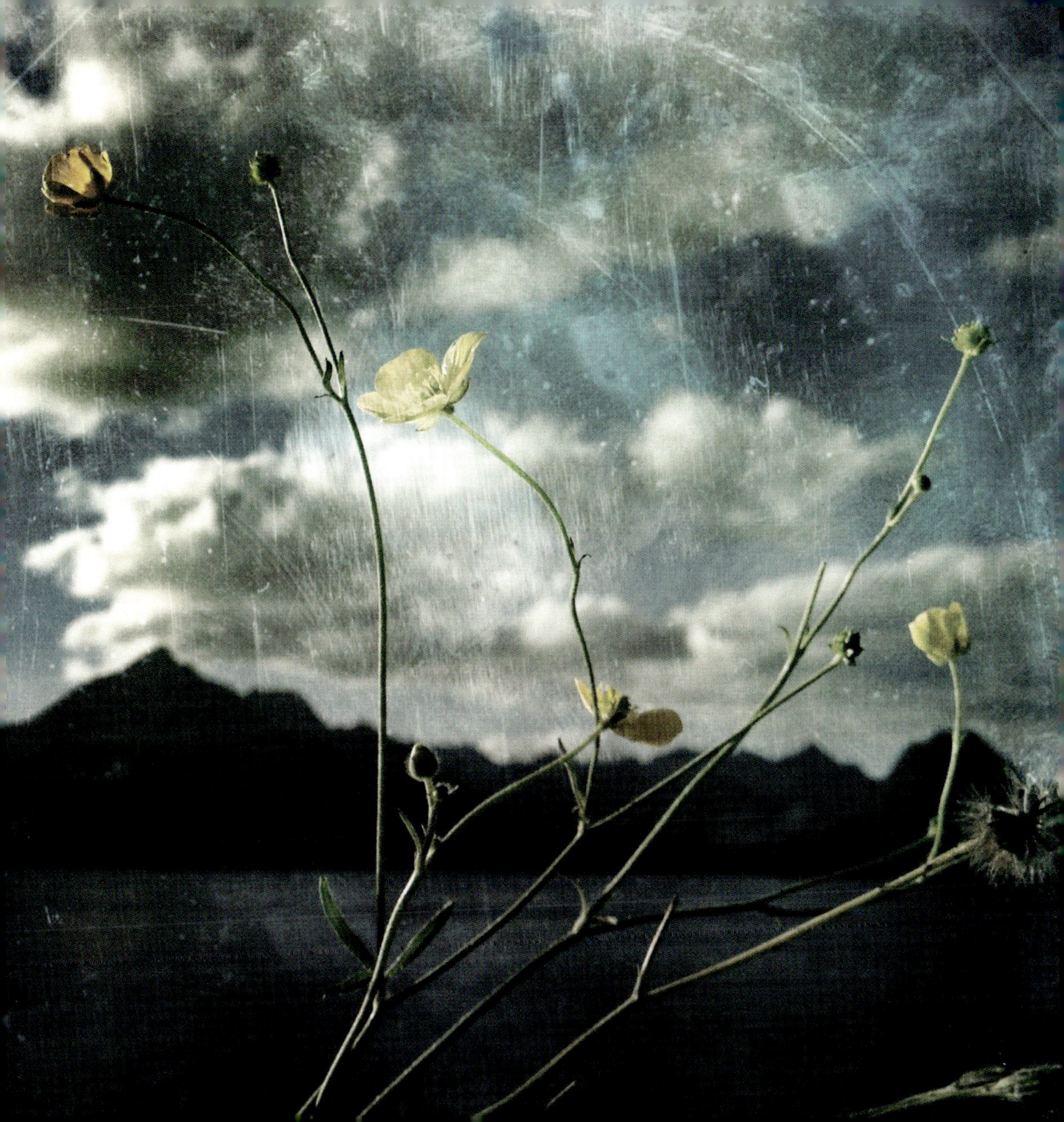

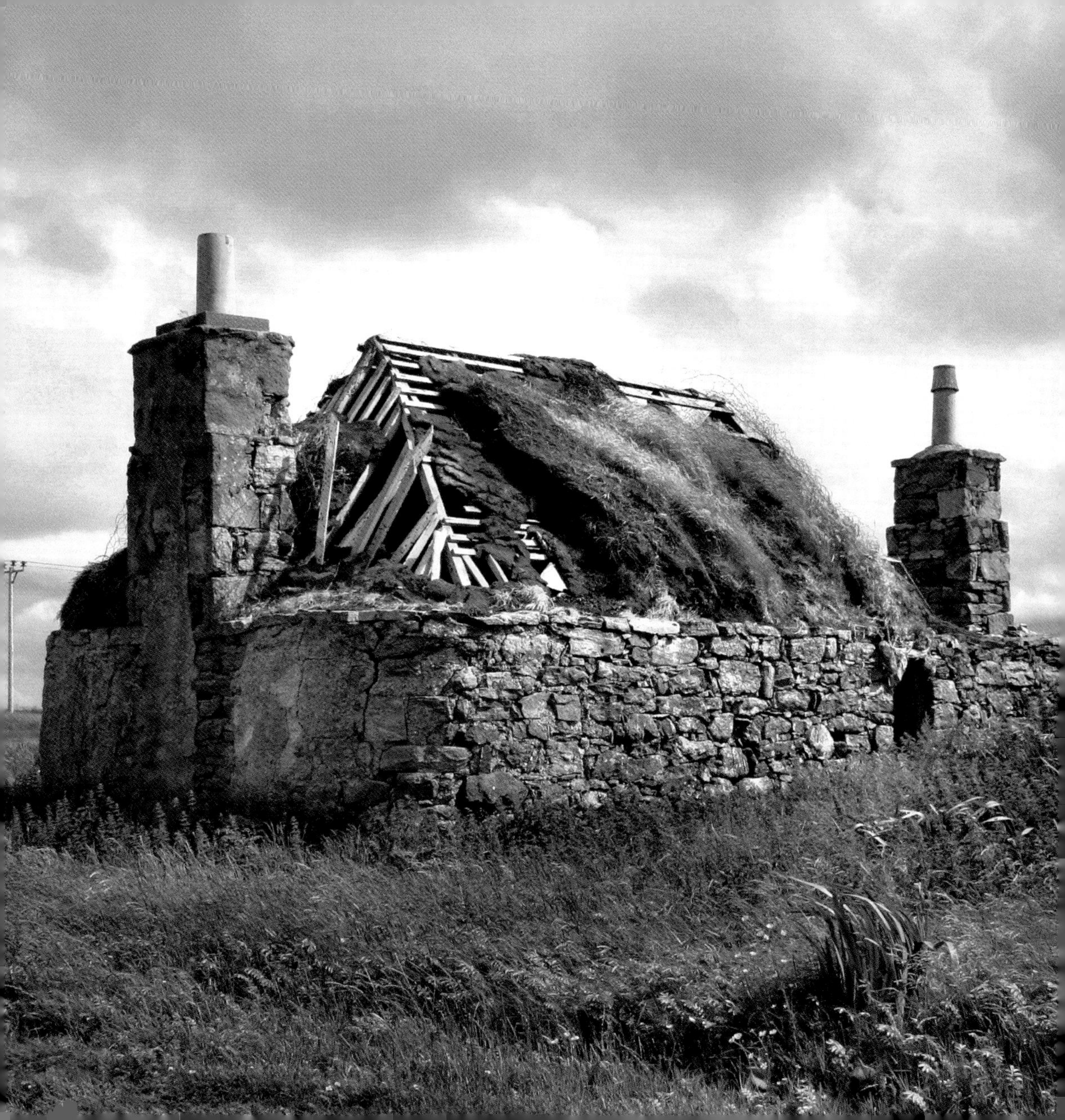

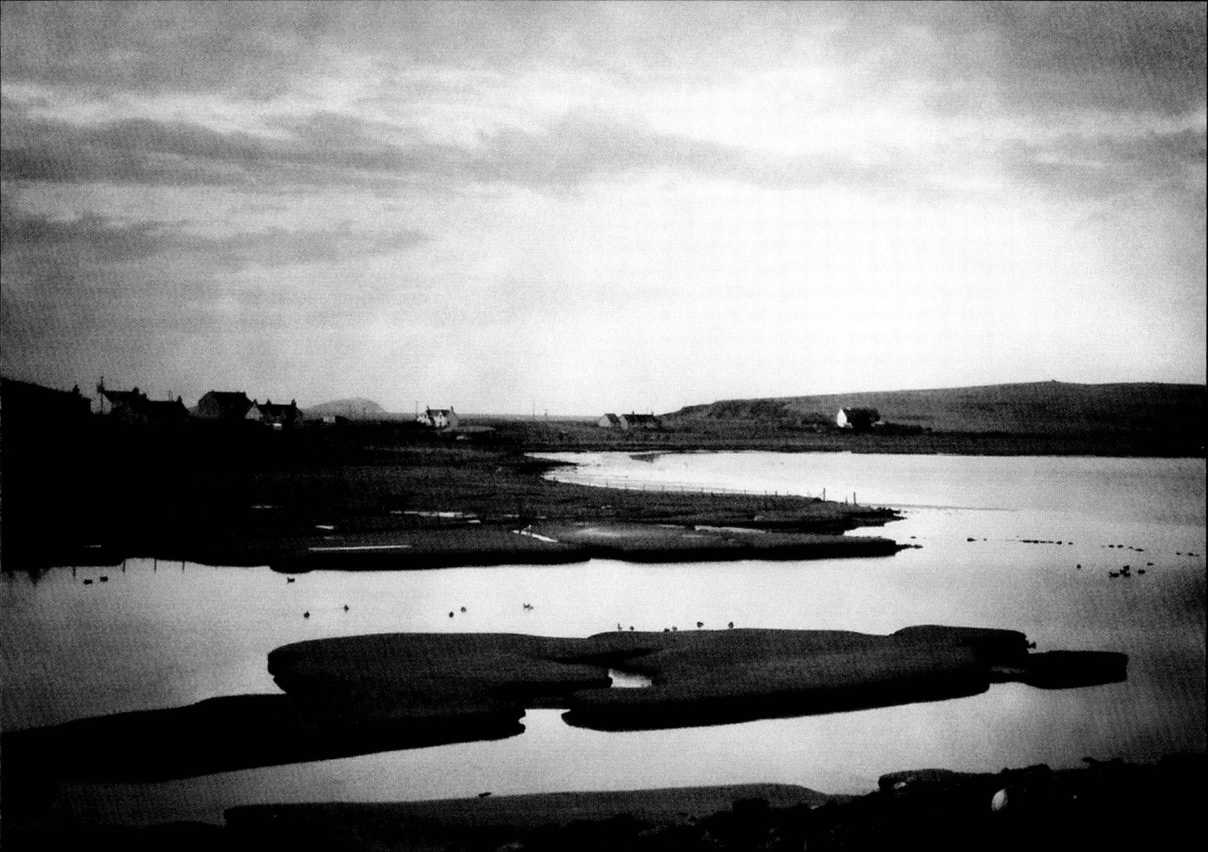

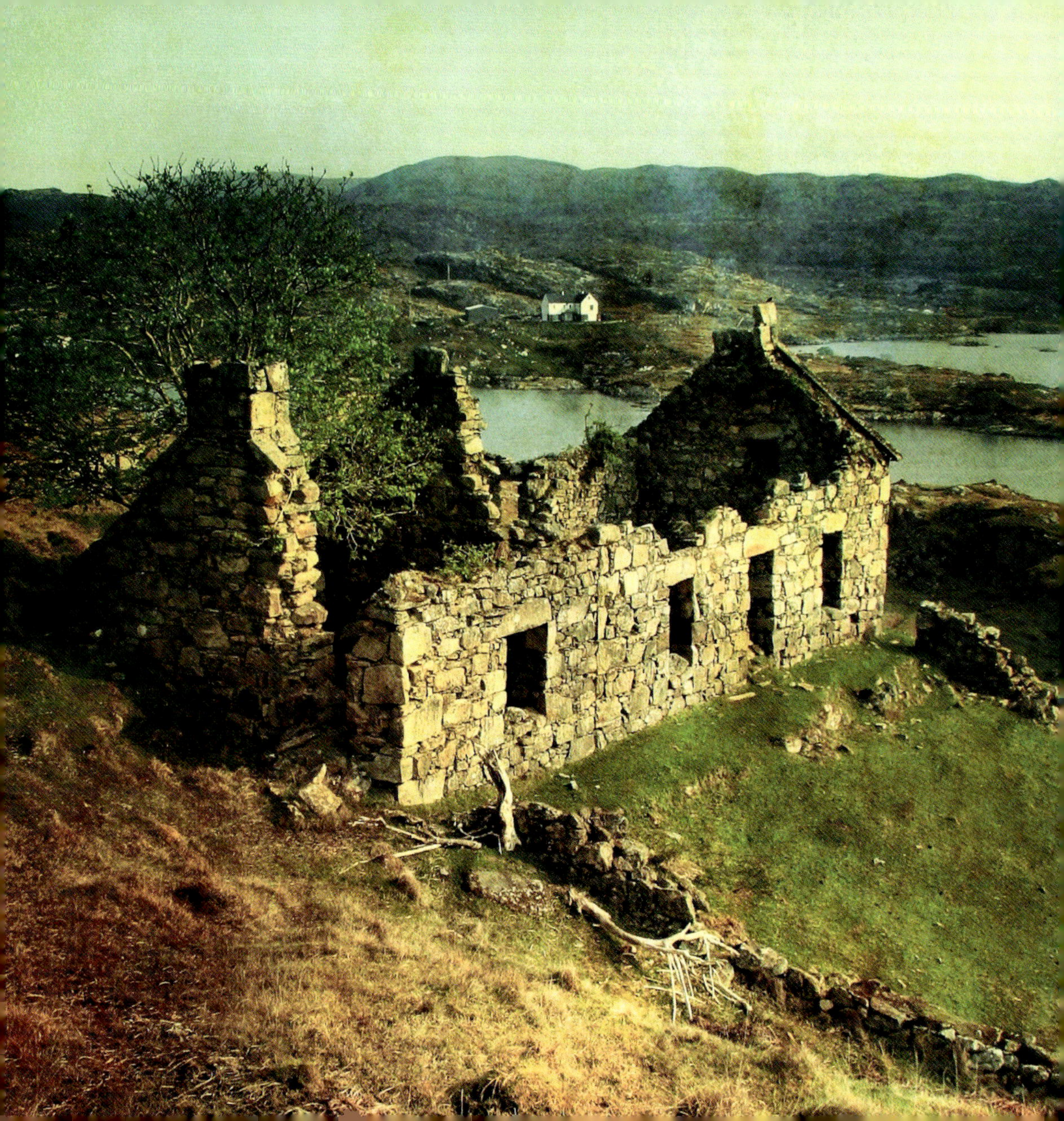

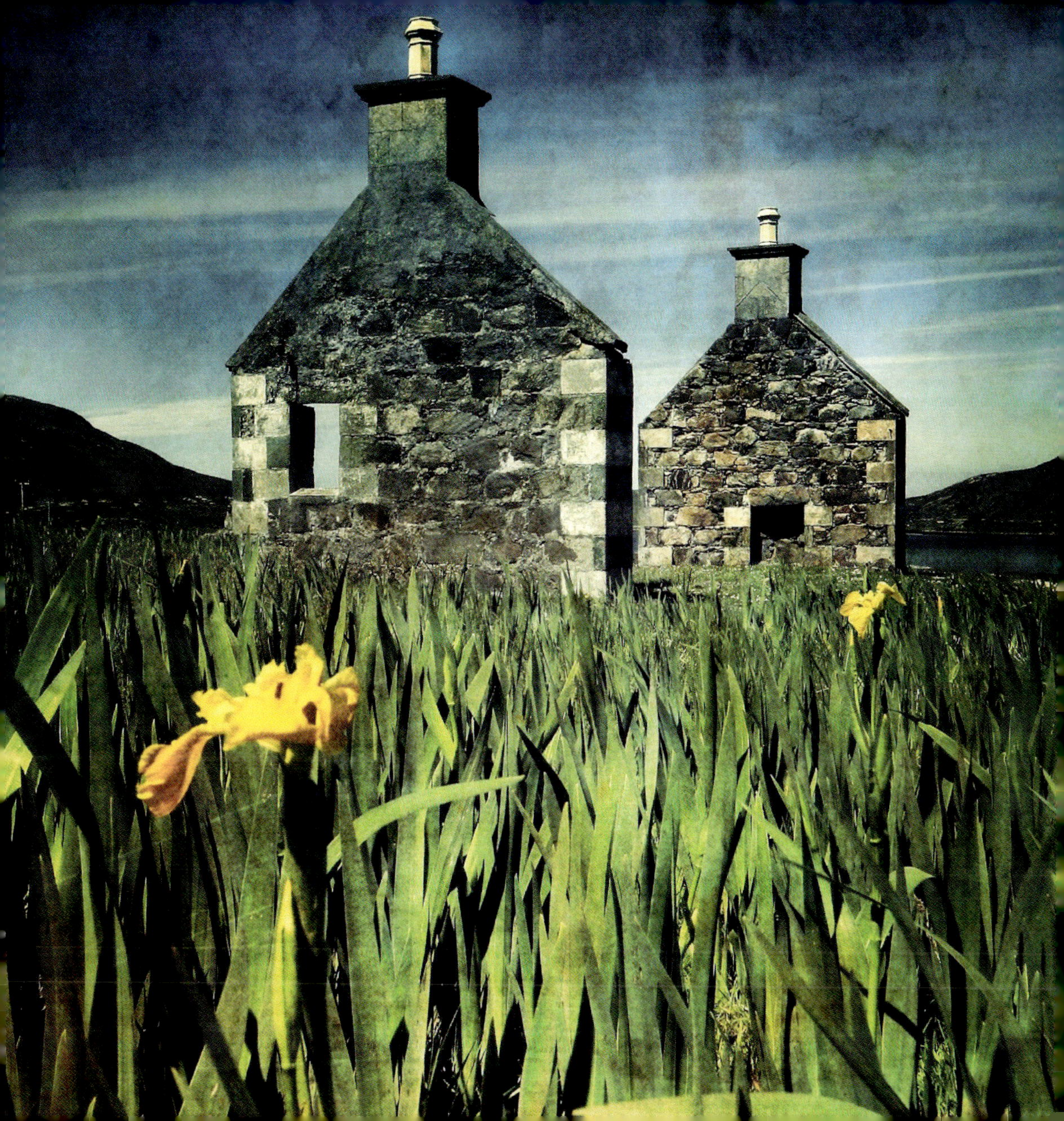

that summer day
the house of elderly ladies
was thrilled
to witness the sail past of the Britannia
a genealogy born in teacups and plates
bore witness
to the sedate
stately waves
reminiscent of a born again
jfk

is it the house that lives in us
or us who live in the house?
the silver polished and burnished in anticipation
the radio crackling
the light programme
interfering and congesting the memory
of a summer royal vacation
newspaper cuttings
fading on the v-lined wall
best hat
best coat
emerging from the mysterious far travelled trunk
releasing serendipity and sixpences
and the distant smell of linen wrapped dumplings
and daffodils
temporarily and chronologically
disordered
in the strangely eclectic
sunshine of the
second
reinvigorated
hall

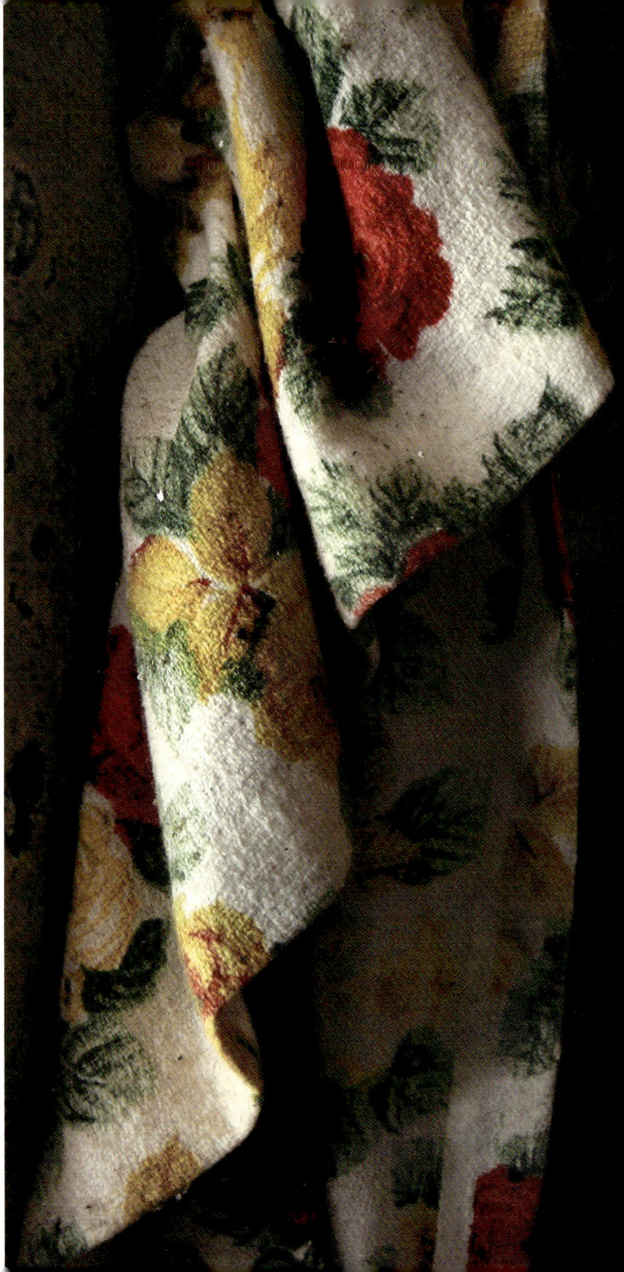

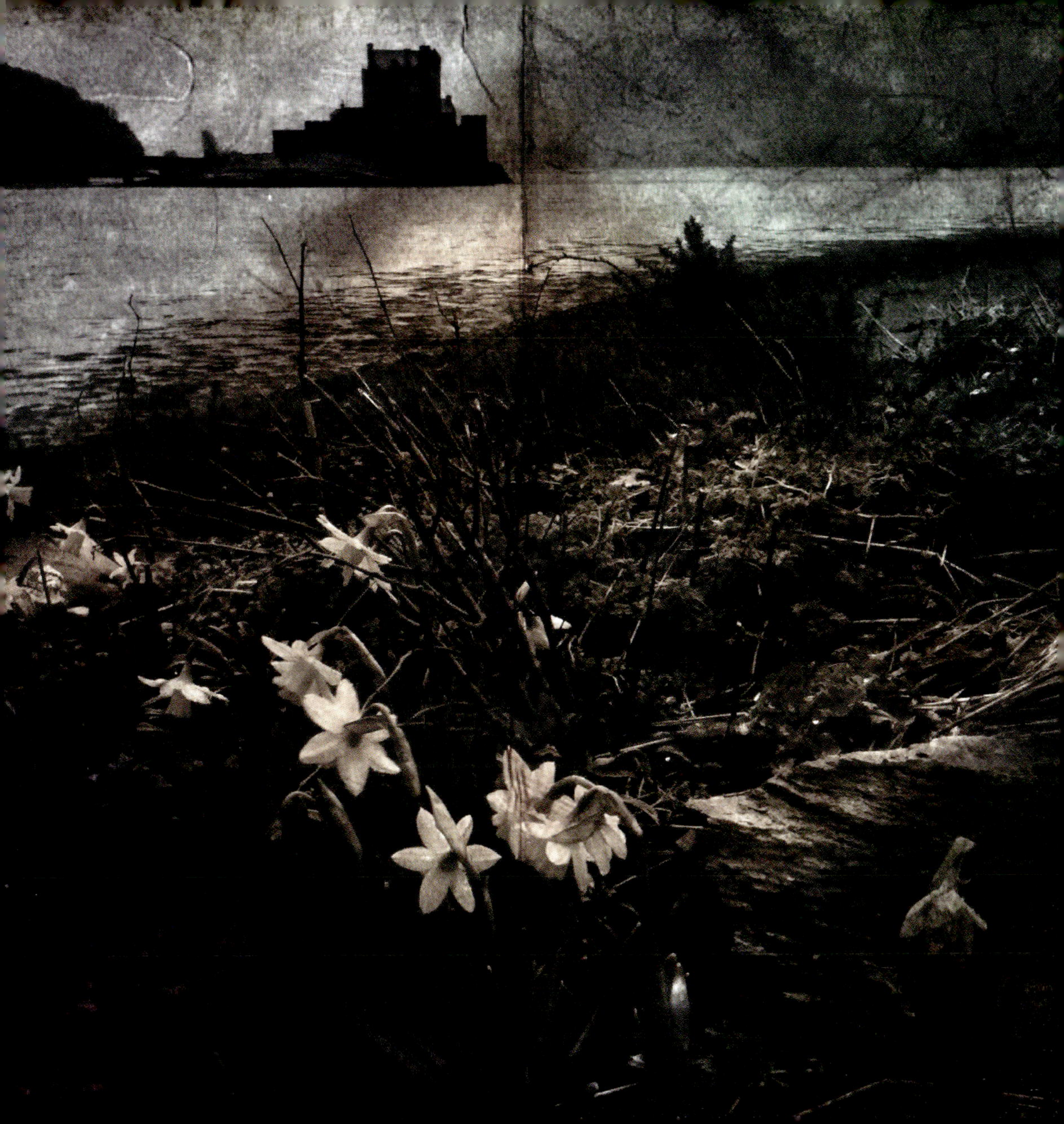

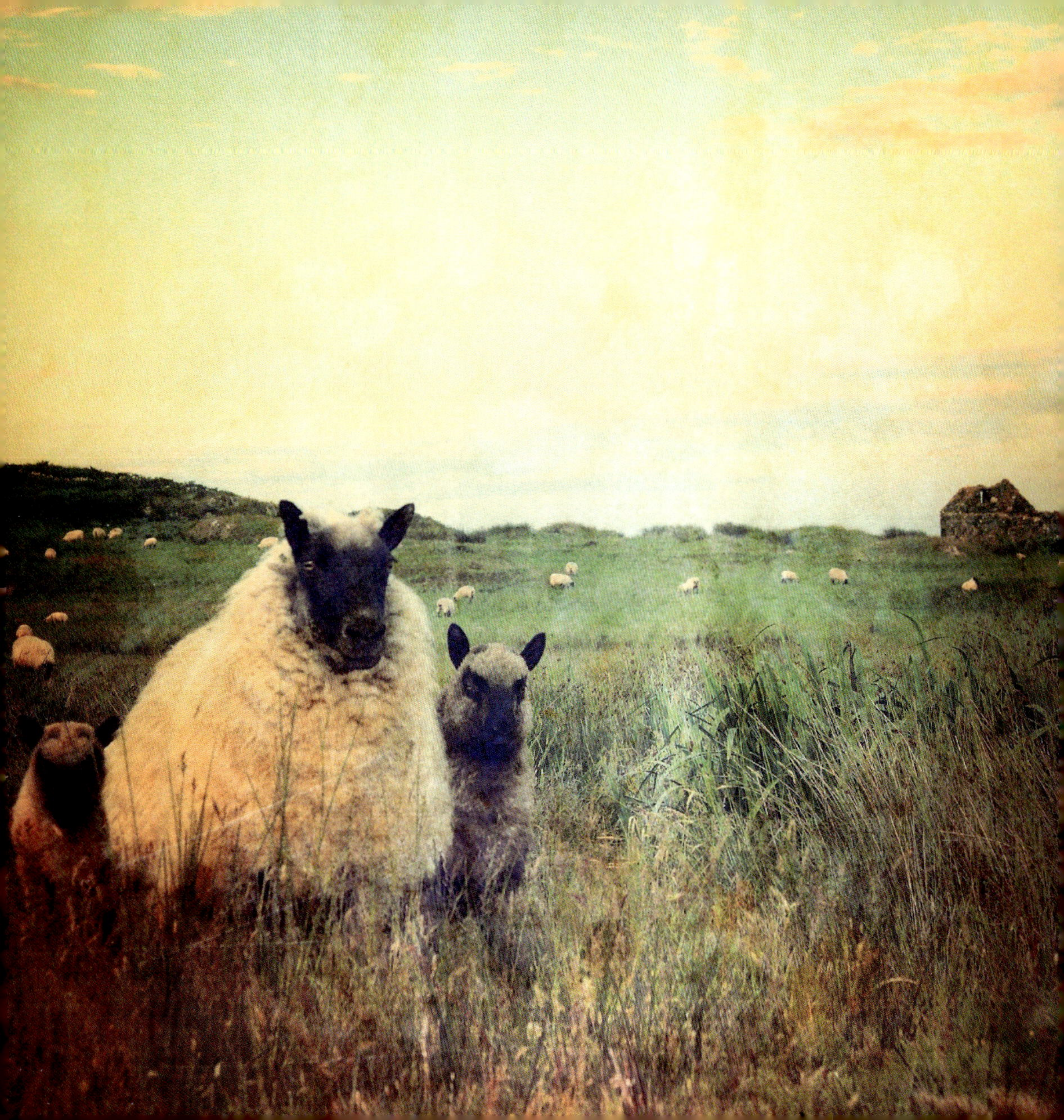

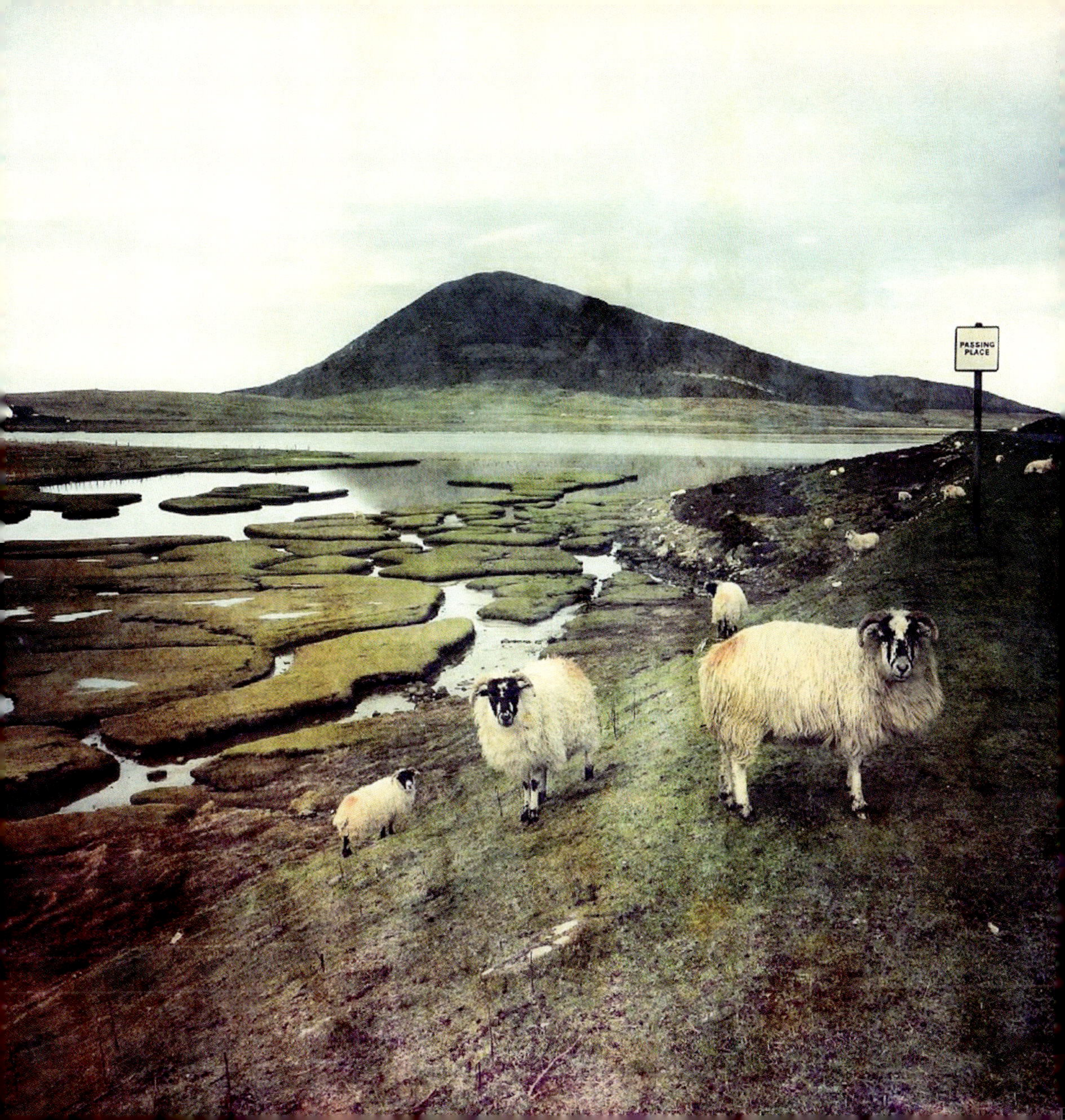
PASSING PLACE

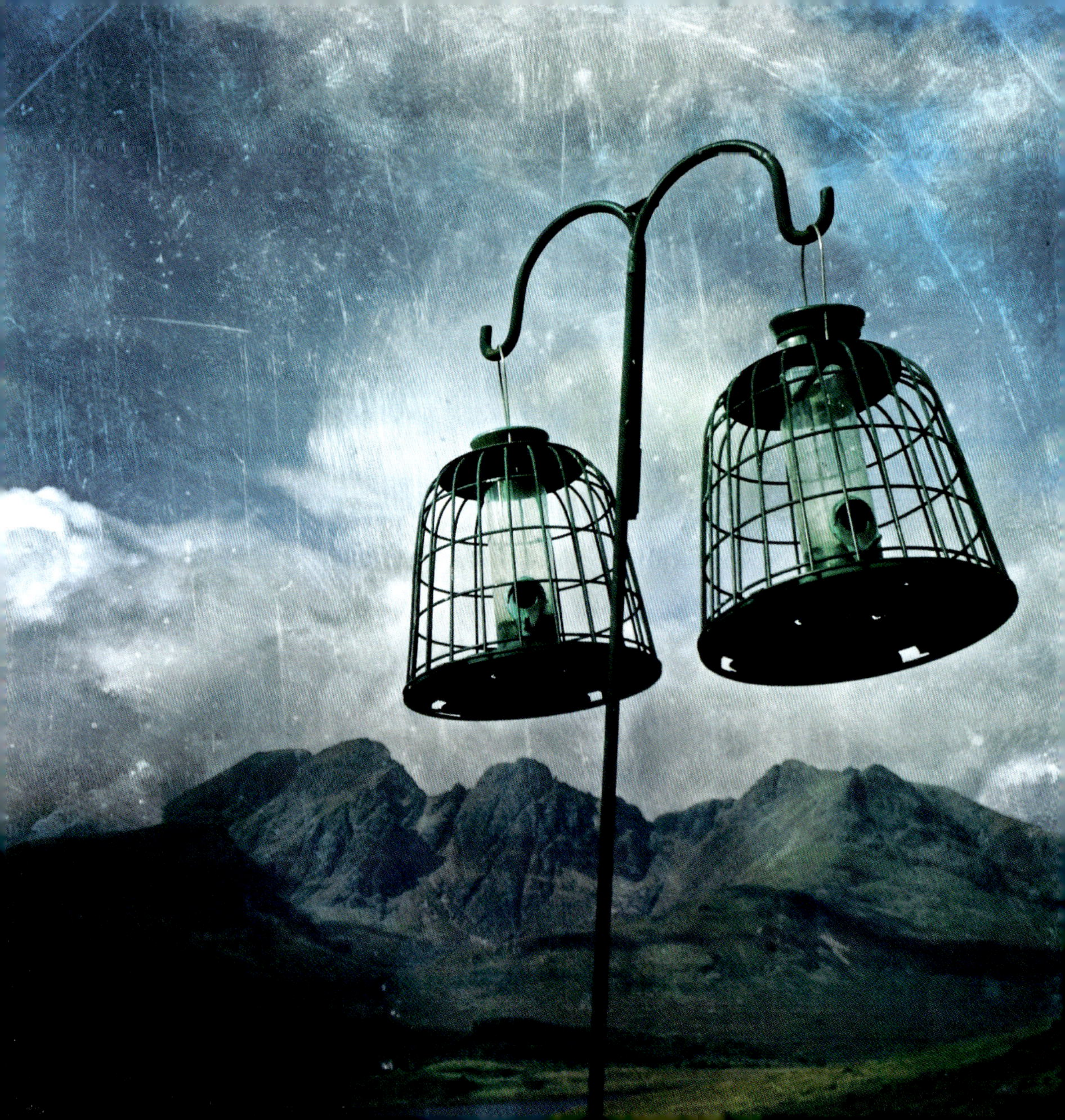

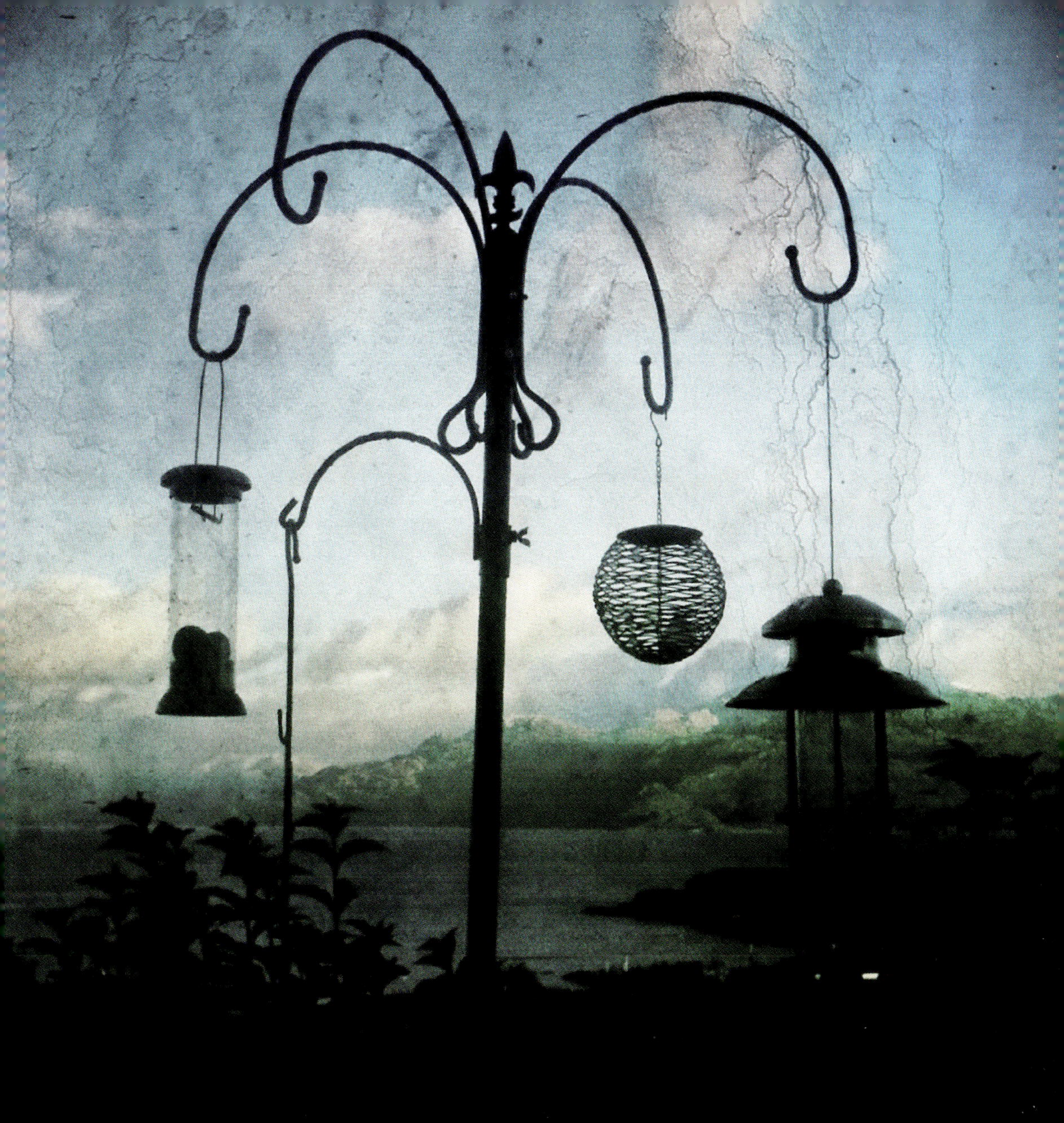

on the faded dresser in the hidden corner
of the forgotten attic
dusty, distinguished, demonstrative
and defiantly out of reach
sits the hourglass
sculpted 70 years last
from that magical bottle of messages
found in the burrow on the dunes
above vatersay west beach

and in a serene newspaper-lined box
an ivory, white-laced tea dress
tightly wrapped, in string and a straight-laced
sunday times typescript, replete
with the inaugural visions of Beveridge and Atlee
lying dormant, asleep
the heartbeats and synchronicity of our VE day
waltz
waiting to be unwrapped
and the eloquent stratigraphy of first love
compressed and protected in its fold
silently
but with a hint and a twinkle, so cajoling and bold
requesting release

with the spectral light of a single candle
and that distant forget-me-not music returning to
my ears
we waltzed once again
your dress sparkled with graceful silhouettes
in the flickering time-denying light
turning back the empty years
to that unforgettable La Carno night

i inhaled your perfume in the teardrop on my
cheek
and smiling, i returned the dress to its box
my tears newly accumulating in the hourglass,
settling in gentle layers in the bottle from
vatersay beach

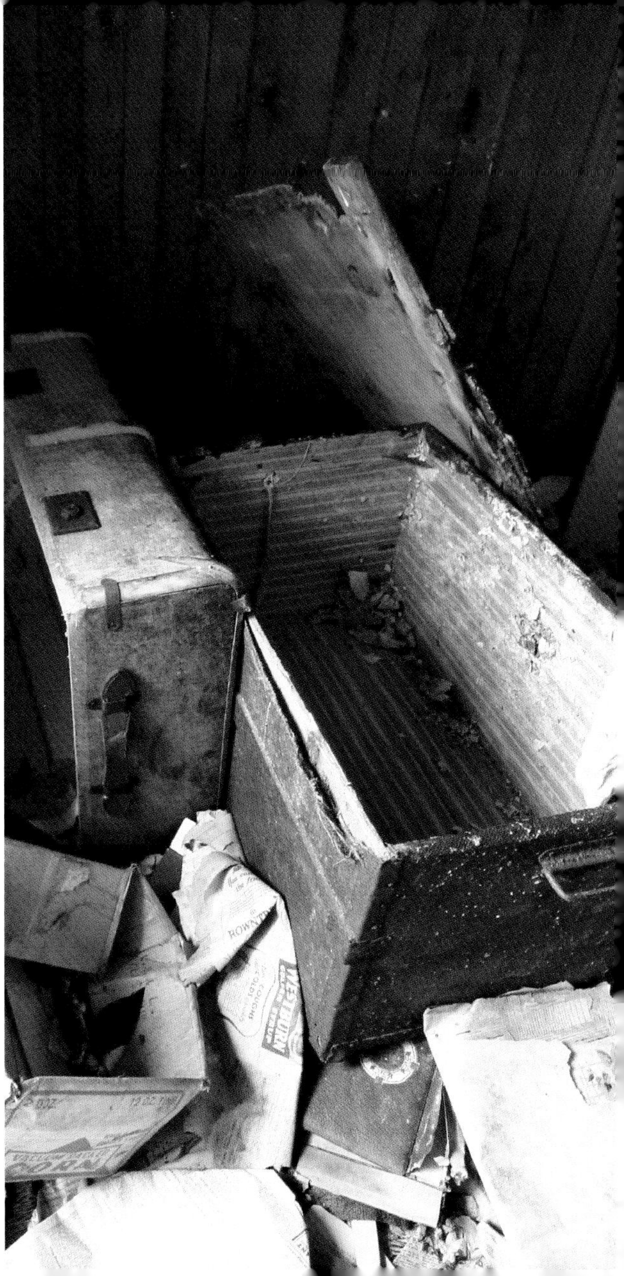

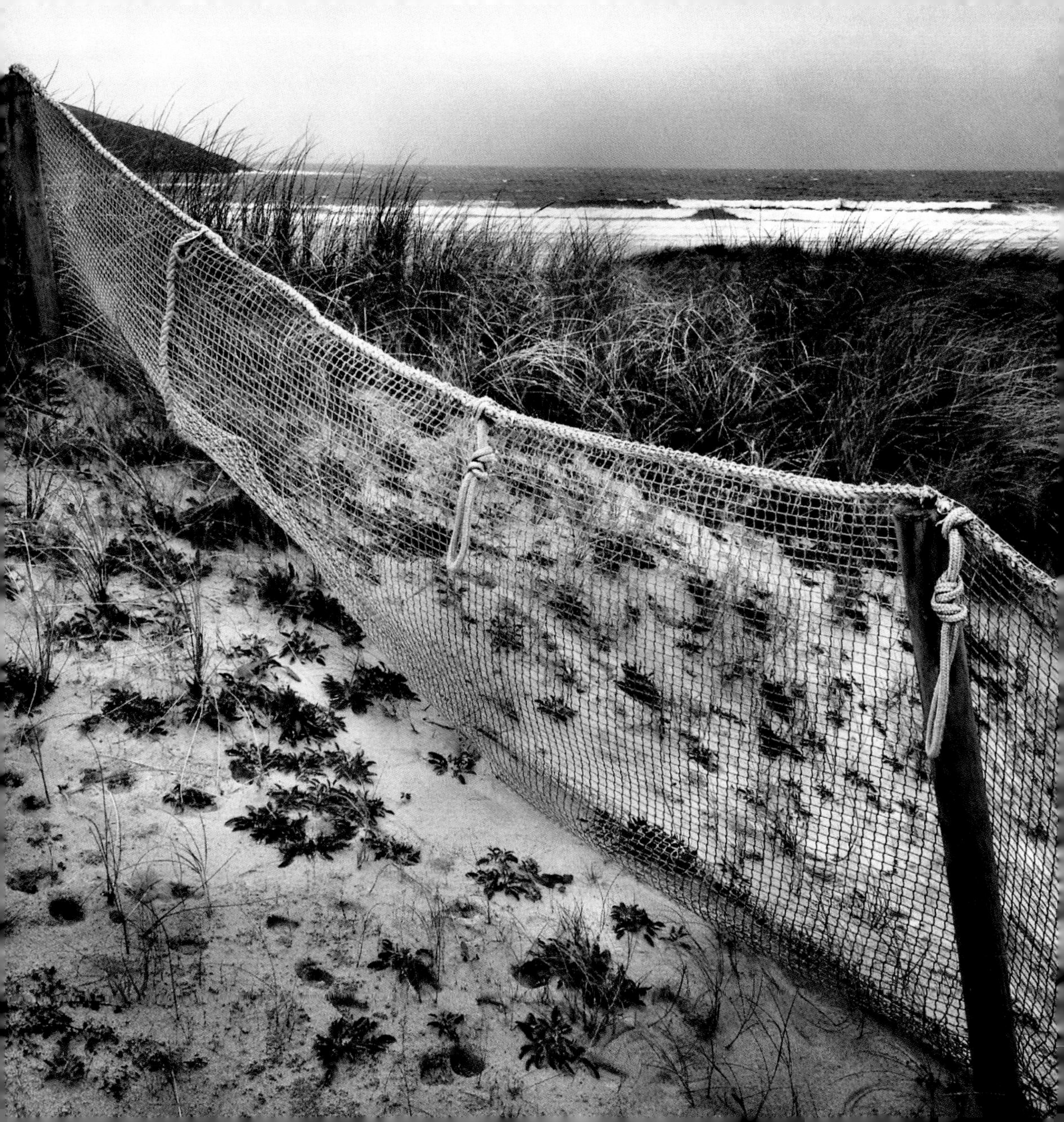

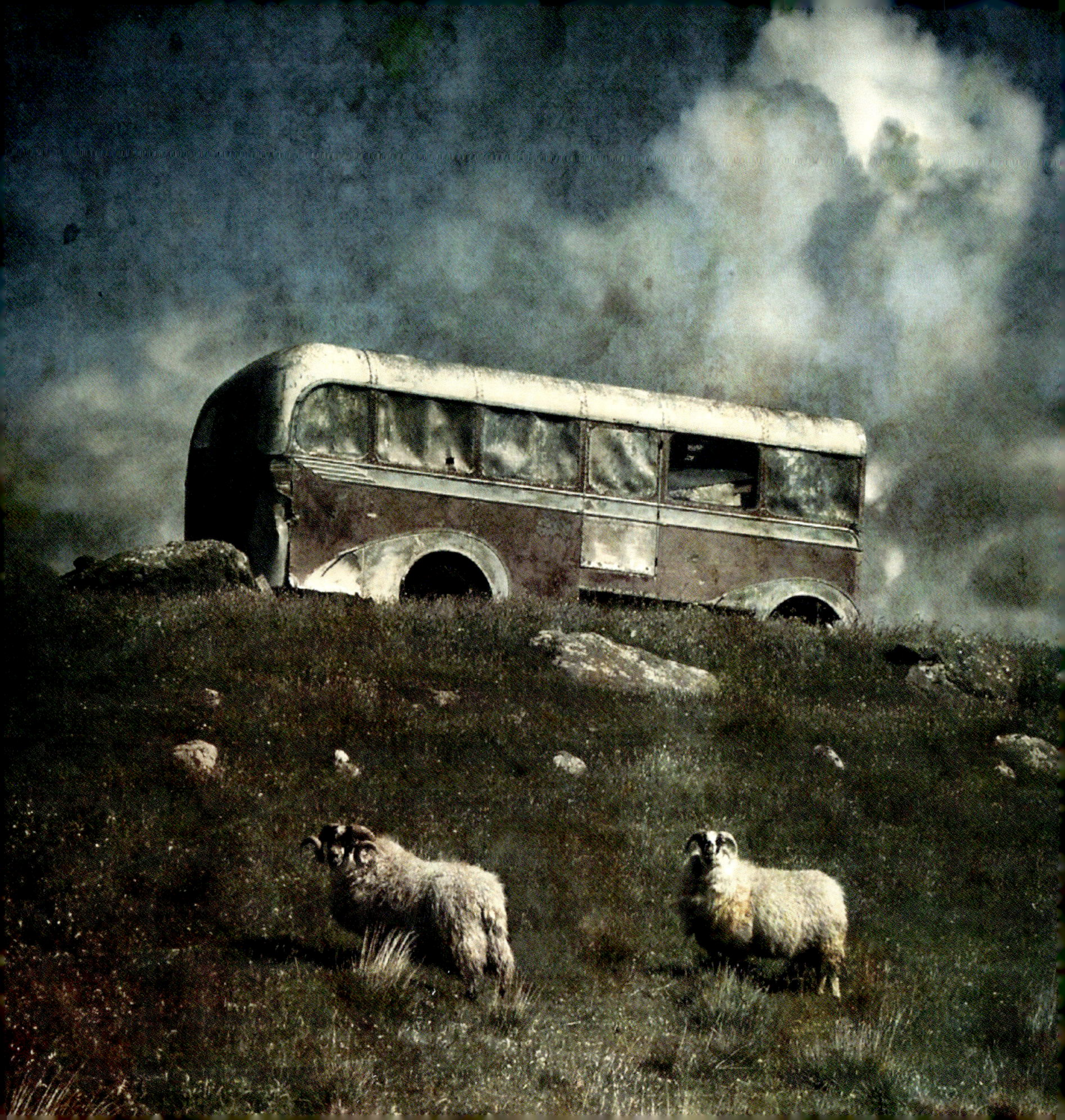

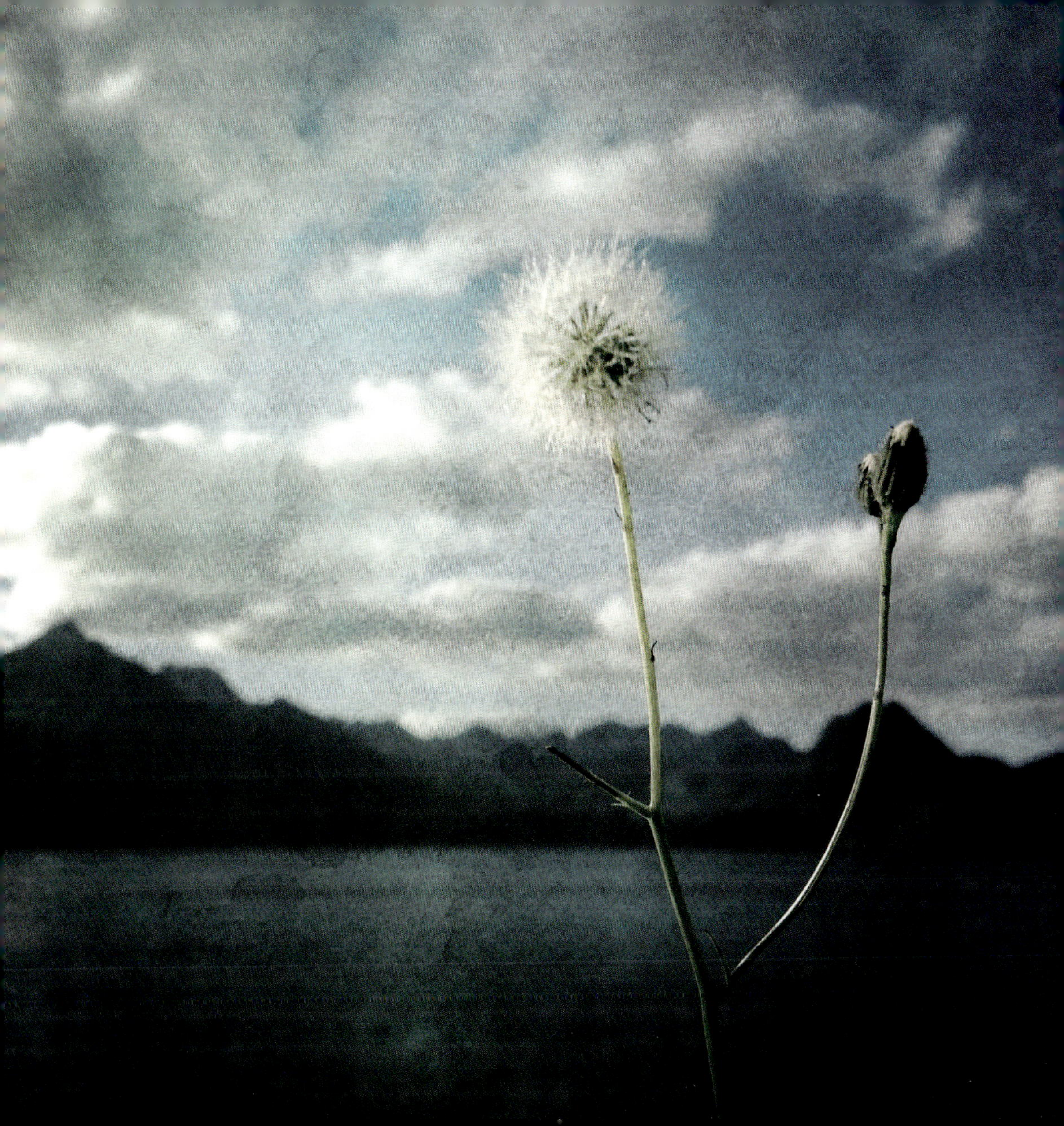

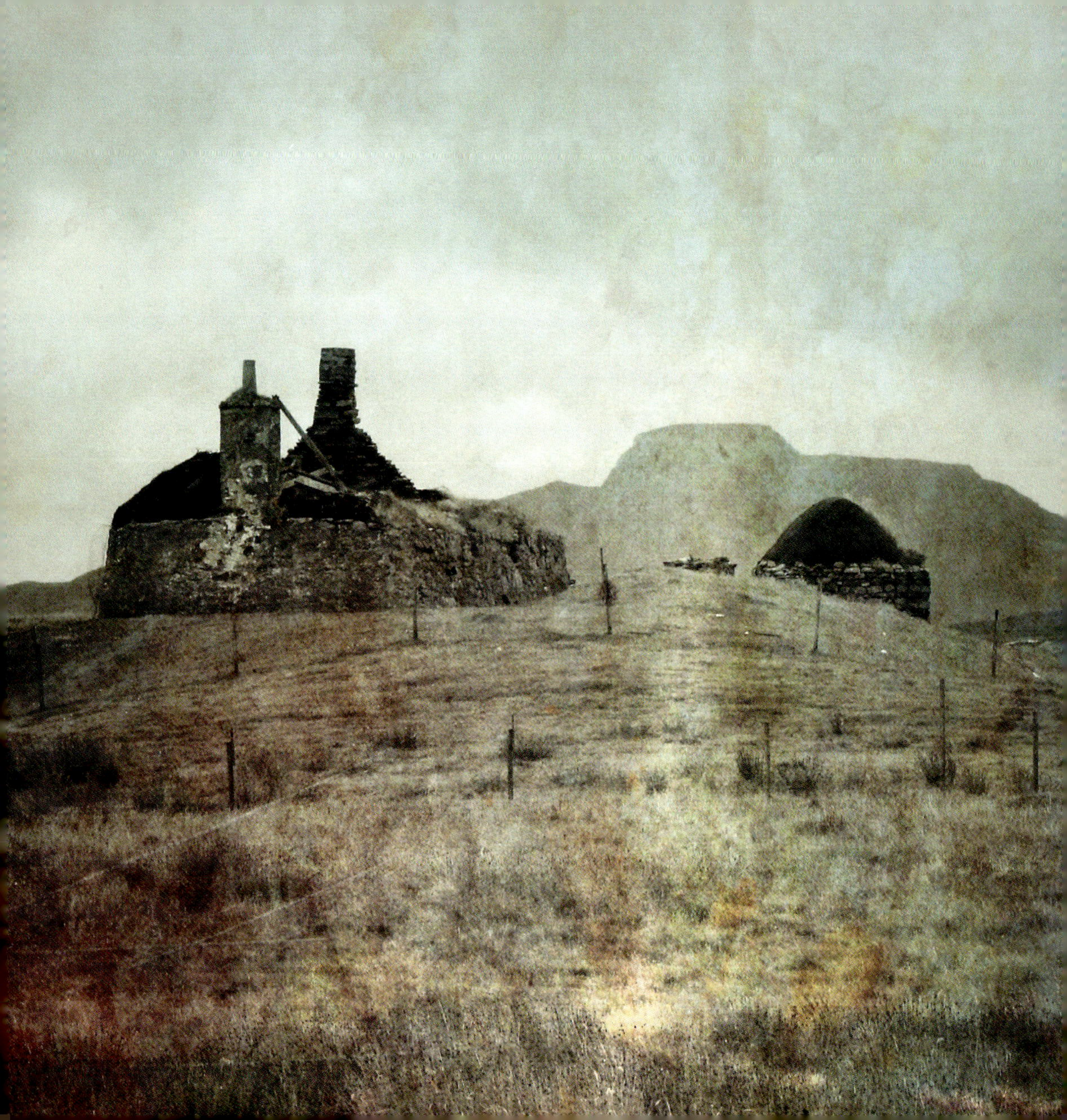

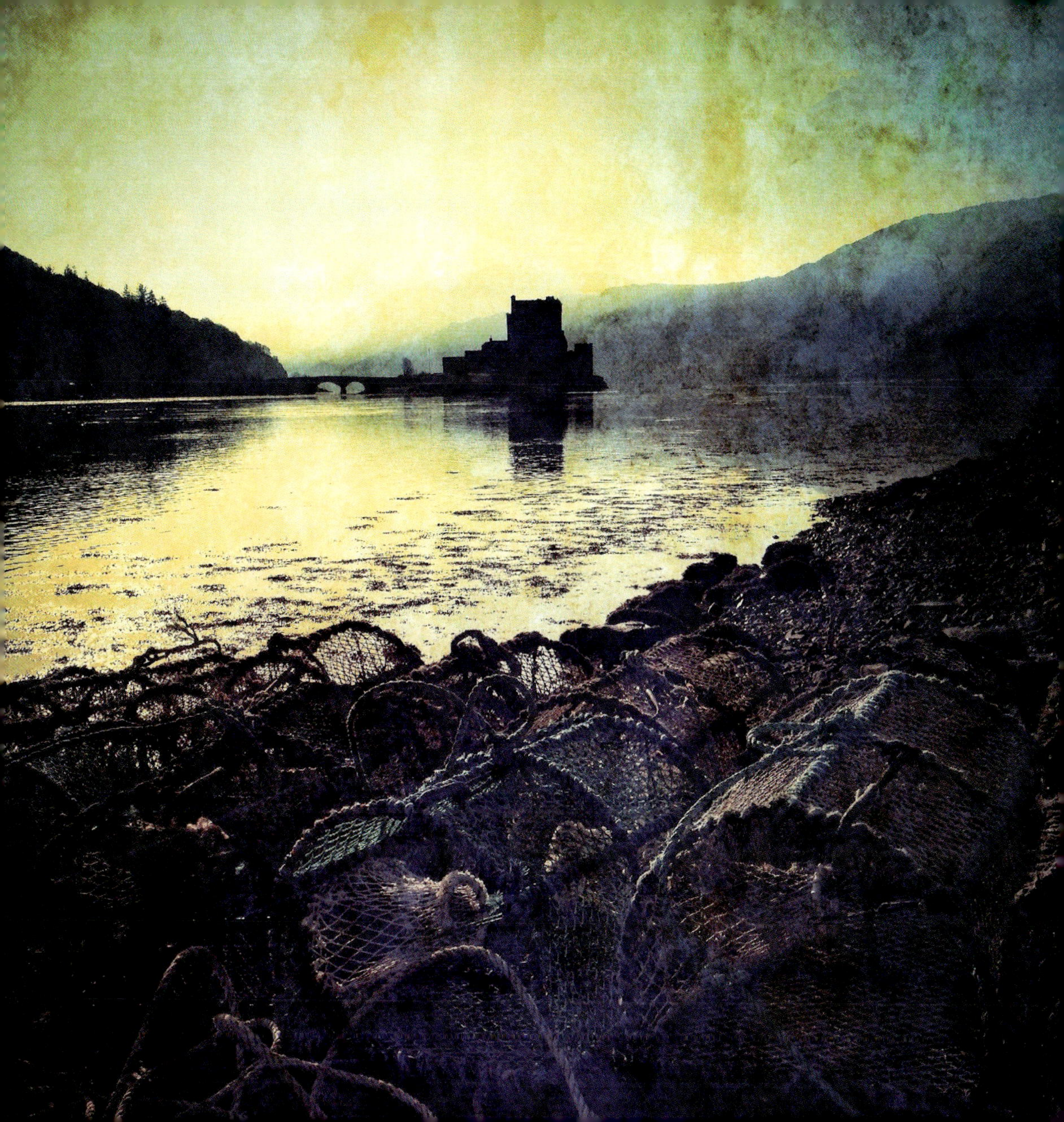

that last morning
after the teacups and the scone
with hesitation
and silent feelings of introspection and a haunting melancholic sense of wrong
breathless,
in clinging claustrophobic ceremony
i closed the curtains
on this chapter of the book
to stop the sun from tarnishing the memories
of laughter and family song

the action encapsulated art and artifact with resilient emotion
denying disturbance from the future robber trenches of the mind
curtailing argument about interpretation
replacing intellectual conflict and commotion
with a knowing devotion
to the architectural material senses
that reveal the soul

the door was sealed in traditional wax red
and the heartbeats and chatter were weighted and stratified in the
twists of the lead

and time
passing time
delivered a garden undemarcated from the moor
the windborne seeds with a calmness so pure
delivered a Lazarus tree
uninhibited and free
and with a smile
born of realisation anew
a steadfast confidence
that the home remains sure
and bold
and true

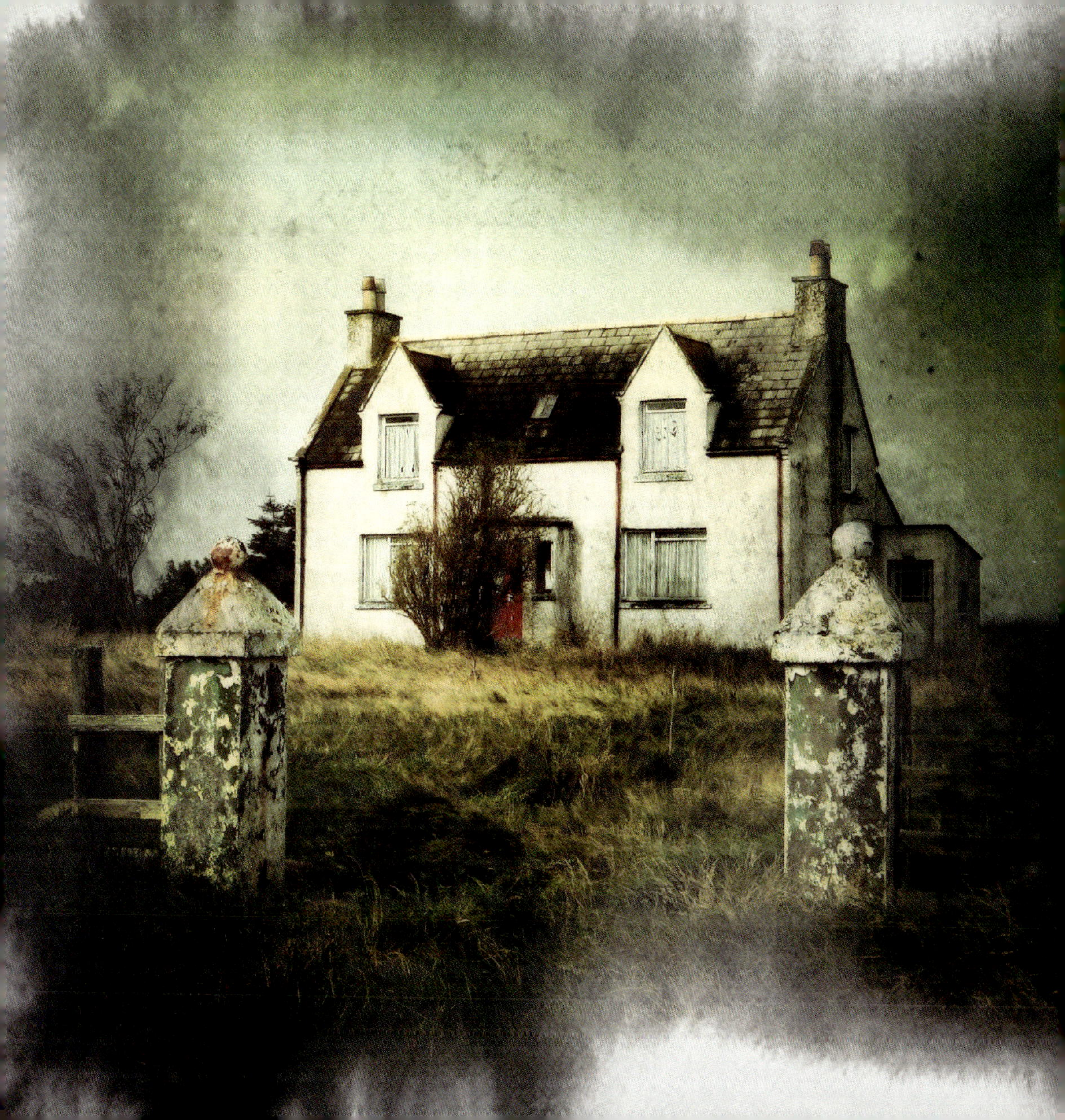

blurb